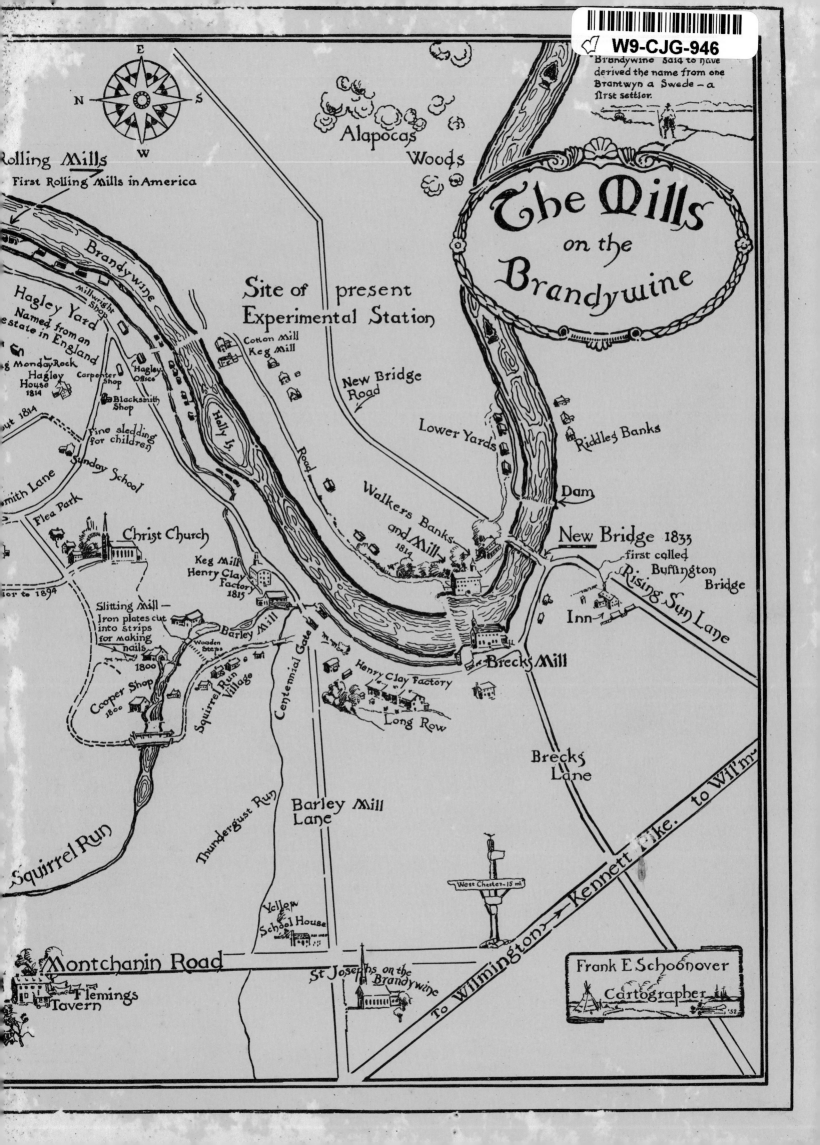

The Mills on the Brandywine

Brandywine said to have derived the name from one Brantwyn a Swede — a first settlor.

Alapocas Woods

Rolling Mills
First Rolling Mills in America

Brandywine

Millwright Shop

Hagley Yard
Named from an estate in England

Big Monday Rock

Hagley House 1814

Carpenter Shop

Hagley Office

Blacksmith Shop

Fine sledding for children

Smith Lane

Sunday School

Flea Park

Christ Church

Site of present Experimental Station

Cotton Mill
Keg Mill

New Bridge Road

Holly Is.

Road

Lower Yards

Riddles Banks

Walkers Banks and Mill 1814

Dam

New Bridge 1833
first called Buffington Bridge

Rising Sun Lane

Keg Mill
Henry Clay Factory 1815

Slitting Mill —
Iron plates cut into strips for making nails 1800

Barley Mill

Wooden Steps

Cooper Shop 1800

Squirrel Run Village

Centennial Gate

Henry Clay Factory

Long Row

Inn

Brecks Mill

Brecks Lane

Squirrel Run

Thundergust Run

Barley Mill Lane

West Chester-15 mi

To Wilmington

Kennett Pike. to Wil'm

Yellow School House

Montchanin Road

Flemings Tavern

St Josephs on the Brandywine

Frank E Schoonover
Cartographer

DU PONT

THE AUTOBIOGRAPHY OF
AN AMERICAN ENTERPRISE

THE STORY OF E. I. DU PONT DE NEMOURS

& COMPANY PUBLISHED IN COMMEMORATION

OF THE 150TH ANNIVERSARY OF THE

FOUNDING OF THE COMPANY ON JULY 19, 1802.

E. I. DU PONT DE NEMOURS & COMPANY

WILMINGTON, DELAWARE

ELEUTHÈRE IRÉNÉE DU PONT

(1771-1834)

FOUNDER OF E. I. DU PONT DE NEMOURS & COMPANY AND PRESIDENT, 1802-1834

PAINTED FROM LIFE BY REMBRANDT PEALE

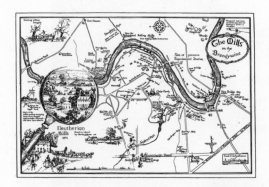

THE MAP

The decorative map inside the front and back covers was drawn especially for this book by Frank E. Schoonover, Wilmington artist. Like his friend and teacher, the late Howard Pyle (see page 17), he is a distinguished illustrator whose works are found in the books and periodicals of many lands.

"The Mills on the Brandywine" represents some exacting on-the-spot research, supplemented by studies and reconciliations of long-forgotten plots, deeds and surveys. Although Mr. Schoonover's map is a work of art, it is authentic and accurate to the last detail.

One interesting duty was to orient the place names appearing on early maps with those which came later to reflect the French influence of the du Ponts. Montchanin Road, for example, appears on maps made prior to 1800 as Centre Road. (Anne de Montchanin was the mother of Pierre Samuel du Pont de Nemours.) A small creek formerly known as Husband's Run was apparently rededicated by the French du Ponts as Dauphin's Run. (Today Du Pont people sometimes refer to it in less formal fashion, as it bisects a fairway at an employee golf course.) The Delaware countryside adjusted itself in time to Eleutherian Mills and to a section across the creek which became known as Louviers, after a town in France. On the other hand, E. I. du Pont's "Le Grande Route de Wilmington à Lancaster" is now a U. S. numbered route, and such rural standbys as Chicken Alley and Duck Street have manfully resisted all intrusions.

Mr. Schoonover's scholarly approach has dispelled the confusion caused by this overlapping of cultures. His imposing panorama, telescoping various periods of time into a composite view, brings a special feeling to 150 years of Du Pont activity near the "Great Bend" of one of America's most historic streams.

Table of Contents

Foreword

THIS is a book without an author, just as it is a story without an end.

In the summer of 1802, masons laid the first stones of a small mill on Brandy-wine Creek, near Wilmington, Delaware. Directing the work, his drawings in hand, was a young refugee from French dictatorship, recently arrived in America. The mill was his stake in the future of his adopted land. From that day forward, the venture was to be known by his name: E. I. du Pont de Nemours.

The century and a half that followed saw both venture and nation expand far beyond the narrow borders that confined each in 1802. This growth has been, in each instance, a matter of cause and effect. Du Pont grew because the growing nation's needs and its free traditions encouraged progress. The nation grew because Du Pont, and a thousand others, were contributing the seeds of growth that germinate in daring, risk and innovation.

Generations of men and women played their parts in this development from a single powder mill to a company national in scope and significance. Over the years they have shared heartbreaks and despair, as well as the satisfactions and rewards. But the company that has emerged rests, like the nation, on a base finely tempered in the fires of time.

This is not a story to be told by a single pen, secure in the somber perspective of history. It is a story set down over the years, written into the record by the lives of the thousands who have participated, as day followed day. This is their story, as they themselves have enacted it: the autobiography of an American enterprise.

THE WILDERNESS The forest primeval, stretching unbroken for hundreds of miles across the rugged and forbidding barrier of the Alleghenies, typi- fied the challenge of the land to which E. I. du Pont came in 1800. But, to the man with an idea, there was no curb upon daring and vision in the broad sweeping vistas of a young and vital America.

2

LAND OF THE FREE

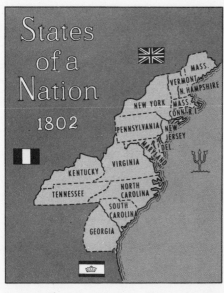

States of a Nation 1802

U.S. of 1802 was made up of 16 States, with Massachusetts split in two. To the north was British Canada; to the west was French territory soon to be bought by Jefferson as the Louisiana Purchase; to the south was Spanish Florida. Area of U.S. was less than 500,000 square miles, half of which was Indian country where settlers were not peacefully welcomed and needed protection.

ELEUTHÈRE IRÉNÉE DU PONT arrived in America on New Year's Day of the year 1800. On that day George Washington had been dead less than three weeks. The national capital was at Philadelphia. John Adams, of Massachusetts, was president; in two years he would be succeeded by Thomas Jefferson of Virginia. Alexander Hamilton was yet to fight his fatal duel with Aaron Burr. Men wore knee breeches, long coats, and three-cornered hats. An American would have to be very young not to remember the marching and countermarching of the Revolution.

America in 1800 was still not so much a nation as a plan for a nation. A string of seaboard colonies, having won independence from England, had, after some years of bickering, united under a Constitution. Not all of the 5,300,000 Americans of the day were enthusiastic about their new Federal Government. Some, like Hamilton, felt it should have greater power. Most, however, agreed with Jefferson "that government governs best that governs least." But the mould of the future had been cast: America was to attract men like du Pont because the principle of individual liberty had been won and written into the bond in blood. Invention, enterprise and development were to flower here for precisely the same reasons that they were to wither elsewhere in the world — because they could flourish only in soil enriched by the organic fertility of freedom.

For with a new political principle had been born a new economic credo, so startling that it is, even now, misunderstood over large portions of the globe. This was the concept that the way to get a job done was to offer inducements and incentives for accomplishment. The prevailing notion elsewhere in the world was that necessity was the most efficient goad, so to make men work you must keep them poor. The new idea was to replace the spur with the promise, so that the hope of reward would unleash the energies and talents of men.

The early steps of the new experiment were faltering and diffident. Americans, having fought eight bitter years to sever the British yoke, were debating how much of their new freedom to trust to the hands of their new government. The one thing on which they agreed, as written into the Constitution, was the belief that government should exist for the people, rather than the people for the government, as was customary elsewhere.

But in those days, as now, Americans had more to do than ponder government. They had livings to make. Seventy-five per cent of them did it by farming. Most farmers raised an assortment of food for their tables and those of nearby towns, though tobacco and rice had already become large money crops. Cotton was coming to be important too, thanks to the demand set up for it by the invention of power-driven textile machinery and of Eli Whitney's cotton gin to prepare fiber. These were making cotton goods cheaper and available to all—and giving Americans their earliest lesson in the fact that industrial progress means benefits to everyone.

The 25 per cent of Americans who were not farmers were small craftsmen (Paul Revere was a noted copper- and silversmith, and Benjamin Franklin had been a printer) or they were professional men, tradesmen, merchants or seamen. The prestige and adventure of military life attracted many.

The big urge in America was to expand and develop. All this meant that the new nation had important things to offer the man of enterprise.

One of these was a literally unbounded market for manufactured goods. It was the mother country's attempt to monopolize that market for itself that had stirred the Revolution.

Another was the spirit of adventure that filled the young nation, providing the climate in which enterprise was at home. Americans had written and backed up their Declaration of Independence, invented an entirely new form of government, and were even now pushing over the Appalachian barrier. A breed that dares such things finds it natural to risk the building of factories and roads and canals and trading ships.

It was in this atmosphere of freedom and daring that Eleuthère Irénée du Pont was presently to found, on Brandywine Creek, a company whose growth was to be bound up forever with that of the vigorous new nation.

AMERICAN SCENE OF 1800 WAS LUSTY,

AMERICAN industry in 1800 had yet to raise the living standard of the average person much above what it had been for centuries. The few industrial employees of the time fell into three groups: "workmen," paid about 65 cents a day; "upper workmen," corresponding to today's foremen and paid about 90 cents a day; and "head work-men," equivalent to modern superintendents, who earned as high as $1.15. Even with money worth many times what it is now, such pay bought few luxuries. Educated men and women were rare, though most country districts had public schools where a child could learn to "read, write, and cipher." City schools sometimes added such elegancies as

Home life was busy since practically everything was homemade. Here woman rolls pie crust; other women tend open fire, spin yarn, churn butter. Only small-est children are spared household chores. Note crude toys with which they played.

Agriculture, occupation of 75 per cent of all Americans, was primitive. Grain was sown by hand, harvested with scythes and threshed by crude flails.

Schoolhouses were located in most populated places, contained overworked schoolmistress, children of assorted ages. Many states provided free but very elementary education; attendance wasn't compulsory and children left early.

Social life was restricted by hard work, but could be hearty, as with these high steppers. George Washington was an ardent patron of the theater.

CRUDE, EXACTING

history, geography, and even literature. But by the age of 12, most farm children were needed for chores and got to school at most four months a year; the lot of the city child was little better. The growth of industry and individual productivity was in a comparatively few decades to provide both the funds for schooling and leisure to make use of it.

The ship *American Eagle* landed du Pont family near Newport, R. I., on Jan. 1, 1800. It took craft 93 days to cross the Atlantic.

Church played important part in people's lives as religious center and as fountain of education. U. S. colleges primarily trained men for the clergy.

Cities in 1800 were small and primitive. New York, above, was second largest city, Philadelphia the first. Bustling waterfront activity was typical in large cities since country depended on imports, and trade was nation's economic lifeblood.

BILL OF MORTALITY,

For Portsmouth, Newhampshire, for A. D. 1802.

BY LYMAN SPALDING, M. B. &c.

COMPLAINT.	AGE.	Jan	Feb	M'h	Ap.	M'y	Jun	Jul.	Au	Sep	Oct	No	D'r.	Total.
Aphtha	4,4 weeks									2				2
Apoplexy	66-33-55-43-63 years	1					1		1		1			5
Atrophy	55-69-40-55,3m. 60years			1								3		6
Cancer	55-63,60 years								1	2				3
Cankerrash	8-2-5,7 m. 2,16,23,4 years								1	1	6			8
Cholera of Infants	6 to 24 months						1	6	2	3				13
Cholic billious	42 years										1			1
Consumption		2	2	4	3	7		1	3		2	2	2	28
Debauchery	55-38 years													2
Dropsy	69-50-84-52,89-24 years	1		1		1			2			1		6
Dropsy in the brain	3-7-7-8-13 years	1	1	1						1		1		5
Dysentery	3,2-2 years							2	1					3
Epilepsy	64-2,2 years							1	2					3
Fever and Ague	33 years								1					1
Fever billious	74-30-27 years		1	1							1			3
Fever billious malignant	44,31,41,13,35,21,39,40,39,13						1	9						10
Fever pulmonic	65,45 years	2												2
Gout	52 years				1									1
Gravel	41 years					1				1				1
Hooping cough	10 weeks to 1 year	3	3											8
Infantile complaints	6 days 4 weeks				1				1					2
Measles	7-1,20,4,9m. 2,7,1,2,1-2 years				1	4	5	1						11
Mortification	7 m. 1 year									1				2
Old age	94,90-78,76 years		2							2				4
Palsy	60-74-64-50 years	1	1									1		4
Phrenitis	30-12 years									1		1		2
Premature birth		2							1					6
Quinsy	3 years													1
Scald head	1 year	1												1
Small pox, natural	33 years													1
Small pox, inoculated	1 year													1
Drowned	48-60 years											1		2
Fall	55 years											1		1
Frozen	82 years		1											1
Poisoned by opium	4 months	1												1
Suicide	32 years													1
Total.		12	10	14	6	17	9	7	24	12	13	12	6	152

Catalog of fatal diseases for 1802 in Portsmouth, N. H., a city of 5600 people, shows poor health facilities and high death rate prevalent in America.

Transportation was difficult for 1800 America. Poor roads made travel risky and slow. Most north-south traffic was by water. Travel in Conestoga wagons took 20 days from Philadelphia to Pittsburgh, was uncomfortable for passengers.

E. I. DU PONT, IMMIGRANT

ELEUTHÈRE IRÉNÉE DU PONT was born in Paris in 1771. During his young life, France had lived under a series of tyrannies, often harsh and always selfish. First had been the ministries of Louis XVI with their crushing extravagancies, taxes and arbitrary powers. Then had come the revolutionary mobs, which took turns guillotining one another's leaders. Finally there came Napoleon, whose dictatorship at home was only thinly concealed by his military victories abroad.

Both young du Pont (he was known as Irénée) and his distinguished father, Pierre Samuel du Pont, were moderate men. As such, they could not feel comfortable in a succession of tyrannical atmospheres. Their very moderation kept them in physical danger from extremists: the son knew what it was to flee in disguise for his life; the father was at one time actually in jail awaiting the guillotine.

Nor was the economic outlook of the family much more promising. Agriculture was the standard way of earning a living, and agriculture, of course, requires land. Bois-des-Fossés, the du Pont estate at Chevannes, sixty miles below Paris, was charming, but small. Both Irénée du Pont and his brother Victor had wives and growing families of children.

In any case, the estate had always been more a family headquarters than a source of income. Pierre Samuel du Pont had most of his life been a "career man" in the government service: he had, among other things, been Inspector General of Commerce in the King's cabinet, and had been raised to the nobility for helping to effect the Peace of Paris between England and the new United States in 1783.

But France now offered little future. Both father and son looked across the sea toward America.

French political climate before, during and after Napoleon was harsh and oppressive. Little existed to encourage a man with an idea. Nation's energies were drained to support Emperor's reckless military adventures.

European economy was strictly controlled by state agencies, which abolished competition by granting monopolies to court favorites. Manufacture of staples like salt, above, was rigidly limited by the tax structure.

Fancy clothes were sure sign of wealth in Europe where the rich lived very well and the rest lived very poorly and looked it.

D. MURPHY, IMMIGRANT

ON the day that Irénée du Pont decided to cast his lot in America, another young man reached a momentous decision. His name was David Murphy. He lived with his father in Brandywine Hundred, near Wilmington, then a town of 3500 souls. He worked on nearby farms.

Like Irénée du Pont, David Murphy had looked to America as the hope of his future. Setting out from his native County Cork he had arrived in Delaware after the Revolution. The new world, although far more abundant than the Irish countryside, was not wholly hospitable. With the limited agricultural tools of the day, scarcely changed since the days of the Caesars, a man needed land to support a family.

On the day that Irénée du Pont settled his own question, David Murphy told his father he was leaving home—for good.

What he was going to do, he didn't yet know. He was, of course, free to do what many Americans in his situation were doing: join the march to the unsettled lands beyond the mountains. Many had succeeded in setting up farms and even frontier towns. Others had fallen prey to Indians, disease, loneliness, or exhaustion. To Murphy, anxious to marry and found a family,* it was a bleak prospect at the turn of the century.

Good land was no longer to be had for the taking. Most of it had already come into the hands of "land companies." Some were honest and fair in their prices, but others existed chiefly to extort from the prospective settler the last bankrupting penny.

Opportunities in business were few for a man with little education. Crafts were learned in apprenticeship, and in boyhood. David Murphy's future, the day he left home, was uncertain indeed.

U. S. political climate was far different from Europe's. Insistence on freedom led to Declaration of Independence, above, and to the American Revolution. With freedom so hard-won, no American would give it up.

Plain clothes were the hallmark of Americans, who mixed freely. Aproned artisans and bewigged merchants were equals.

U. S. economy encouraged initiative, and craftsmen, such as these gunsmiths, were setting up shop. In France, few had opportunity to better their station in life, while in U. S. the door of advancement was open to all.

*The Census of 1810 shows this ambition realized. The David Murphys reported a boy and two girls. A year later, Murphy became a U.S. citizen in the Delaware District Court. E. I. du Pont's naturalization papers date from 1804.

Benjamin Franklin, 1706-1790, helped to draft the Declaration of Independence, was America's first great scientist and diplomat.

James Madison, 1751-1836, was the architect of the Constitution and fourth president of U.S. He headed the country during War of 1812.

Robert Morris, 1734-1806, born in England, came to the U. S., where he prospered. He used his fortune to finance the American Revolution.

Adam Smith, 1723-1790, was a Scottish economist whose book, *The Wealth of Nations*, published in 1776, set pattern of U. S. economy.

Benjamin Rush, 1745-1813, physician, taught humane care of insane, signed the Declaration, founded first anti-slavery society.

Patrick Henry, 1736-1799, was the vocal firebrand of the American Revolution, is famous for saying "Give me liberty or give me death!"

Rev. Francis Asbury, 1745-1816, born in England, started Methodist Church here. Pro-American, he refused to accept recall to England.

Washington Irving, 1783-1859, was first important U. S. author, is known for *Rip Van Winkle*, but big work was Washington biography.

IRÉNÉE DU PONT LOOKS TO AMERICA

THE career of Irénée du Pont's father had earned him distinction but little money; with his tendency to moderation his prospects in the French government service were uncertain. His son's outlook was bleaker.

In 1799 Irénée du Pont was making a precarious and not expansive living operating a Paris publishing house. His printing shop, the main source of his income, had once been wrecked by the mob during a political uproar; there was no guarantee that the same thing might not happen again.

A family with its future so uncertain can now look to business for a means of making a living. But in the France of that day there was almost no industry. Much of what there was belonged to the government or ran on monopolies granted to personal or political favorites, and these appoint-

ments had a way of terminating suddenly, as Irénée du Pont had reason to know. Such a change had ended, tragically, what was to be the most important association of his life.

Scientifically inclined, he had as a young man been overjoyed to be apprenticed to the famed French chemist, Antoine Lavoisier,* the greatest scientist of his day, superintendent of the government gunpowder plant at Essonne. Under his careful eye, the boy learned the craft of powder-making, and acquired a precise sense of the scientific method. But Lavoisier's days were numbered. The Revolution struck. On a black day the great chemist, who had served his nation so well, was guillotined. France, Robespierre announced airily, had no need of scientists.

Irénée du Pont approached his thirtieth year with a very real problem. Without political stability, going into business was a risk few would undertake. It was bad enough to be without intellectual independence. He had also a growing family to feed. It is not hard to see why he welcomed going to America, where men were already free to meet that obligation in their own way.

Du Pont family residence in France had carriage house, barns and stables.

*Du Pont first planned to call his plant the Lavoisier Mills, out of respect for his preceptor. Later he changed it to Eleutherian Mills, meaning "freedom," a happy portent to political refugees.

George Washington, 1732-1799, led fight for independence, made Constitution come to life. He saw vigilance as the price of U.S. freedom.

John Jacob Astor, 1763-1848, came to U. S. from Germany. As master of early fur trade he set example of the daring that built America.

Thomas Paine, 1737-1809, born in England, was literary and ideological firebrand of Revolution, zealous foe of tyranny here and abroad.

John Adams, 1735-1826, second president, championed Declaration through Congress, worked hard to get Bill of Rights ratified.

Alexander Hamilton, 1757 - 1804, first Secretary of Treasury, put U.S. economy on sound footing. He foresaw the America of abundance.

Meriwether Lewis, 1774-1809, Jefferson's secretary, led expedition, with William Clark, to the Pacific, helped pioneer the great West.

James Monroe, 1758-1831, was the fifth U. S. president, proclaimed Monroe Doctrine, warning Europe to keep out of Western Hemisphere.

Thomas Jefferson, 1743 - 1826, third president and early advocate of freedom, urged E. I. du Pont to make powder here.

DAVID MURPHY GETS A CHANCE

ACTUALLY, what handicapped David Murphy was lack of capital. He had no funds to buy land or to set himself up in trade. Murphy's resources consisted chiefly of his willingness to work—plus certain farm-bred skills at stonelaying, hammer-and-saw carpentry, and other hand crafts. If only someone with capital and a sense of industrial organization would set up some sort of factory near Wilmington, Dave would be an excellent man to hire.

Dave Murphy's economic frustration betokened no backwardness or servility. He treasured his political freedom, for as an Irishman he had had little chance to enjoy it in his native land. He was proud that his new community was flourishing. Delaware had been the first to ratify the new Constitution; his town, Wilmington, was a small but busy seaport. In his *Mirror of the*

U. S. house,* built before 1800, had 2 rooms. The fireplace was the kitchen.

Times, published at The Sign of Shakespear, Market Street, he could read that the schooner *Eliza* had arrived from New Orleans and the sloop *Industry* from St. Bartholomew. As a result of such goings and comings he could see at John and William Warner's, "Malaga, Port, Lisbon, Teneriffe & Sherry Wines; Coniac Brandy; Excellent Spanish Segars in boxes; Powder & Shot, &c."

But few of the above products concerned Dave Murphy; until he should find a place to work, his fare was slim. Factories being built in America were helping to solve similar problems. They offered few of the benefits now common; pay rarely reached a dollar a day, work ran from dawn to dark, pensions and compensation for injury were unknown. Still, when a man found a good employer, he felt he had struck a good bargain: in return for his work, he got what was for the day a comfortable livelihood. Dave Murphy was soon to meet Irénée du Pont and strike such a bargain. Capital and labor were to unite, under the auspices of management, in a bond that was to make the young nation the busy workshop of the civilized world.

*This house, built on Broom Farm, was occupied briefly by du Ponts while permanent home was built. Earlier, evidence indicates, they lived in nearby log cabin.

Protection from Indians, aroused by white men settling on their hunting grounds, required lots of cheap, dependable gunpowder. U. S. powder was poor, good European powder was expensive.

Coal mining at the Mauch Chunk mines in Lehigh Valley of Pennsylvania—from digging to hauling—was done by hand. Without powder to loose coal and speed work, mine's output was limited.

NEEDED: A BETTER GRADE OF POWDER

NOT long after his arrival in this country, so the story goes, Irénée du Pont bought some gunpowder for a day's hunting.* An expert, he was shocked and disgusted at its poor quality. This surprised no one but him; occasionally good gunpowder came from England for sale at high prices, but for the most part Americans had to get along with poor native imitations. Good gunpowder was a very real necessity to settlers venturing over the mountains. They needed it for protection from hostile Indians, to shoot game for meat and skins, to help clear land of boulders, and to help build roads. Here was an opportunity of the sort businesses are built on: a human need waiting for someone with the skill and enterprise to see that it is filled.

Protection from wild animals was a vital need on the lonely frontier where a weapon was a man's best friend. Though game was abundant, life on the fringes of civilization held numerous perils.

Clearing land for new homes was a long, hard job. Vegetation grew everywhere. Uprooting a tree stump—a matter of minutes with powder—took days, needed two strong men and two horses.

Canal building opened the country to travel and commerce, was a very important factor in America's early growth. It was primarily a hand operation requiring many years of back-breaking labor.

*To fire a rifle of this period, the rule-of-thumb powder charge was 60 grains. This averaged out to about 115 shots per pound of gunpowder. Powder horns held from half a pound to a pound. Later "Du Pont and Galena" (powder and lead) became a standard item on frontier shopping lists.

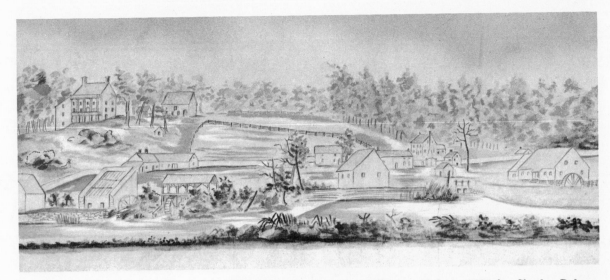

First drawing of powder mills was made in 1806 by Charles Dalmas, du Pont's brother-in-law and a workman in the mills. Beyond the mills were the homes of the workmen and stores to meet their everyday needs.

GOING INTO BUSINESS

IRÉNÉE DU PONT had no thought of gunpowder when he came to America. With his father and older brother, Victor, he hoped to set up a sort of colony in which Frenchmen like himself could start life anew. The colony would contain farms, sawmills to provide lumber for homes and barns, factories to make glassware and pottery, and a suitable complement of schools, churches and stores. Business headquarters of the project were to be near the proposed national capital, Washington, which was just then being built to the plans of another Frenchman, Pierre L'Enfant. The colony itself would be in northern Virginia, "in a beautiful valley above the Shenandoah."

Actually, this plan was just one of a dozen in the elder du Pont's enterprising brain as he reached America's shores. He proposed, for example, to set up a fast mail and passenger service between America and Europe and engage in the trade between France and her colonies in the West Indies and the Far East. To finance his plans, he had set up the firm of Du Pont de Nemours Père, Fils et Compagnie with a proposed capitalization of 4,000,000 francs.

The money was to come from the family and from shares publicly sold at 10,000 francs each. Shares were subscribed by some distinguished Frenchmen, including La Fayette the soldier, Beaumarchais the playwright, and Rousseau the philosopher. But little more than a tenth of the proposed 4,000,000 francs was actually paid in, and it was with this foreshortened capital that the du Pont men and their wives and children assembled in America on the first day of the new century.

They had not been here long when they began to doubt if the Virginia colony plan would ever get off paper. Of the new nation's 5,300,000 inhabitants, over 900,000 were already in Virginia, many of them as land speculators. Prices for suitable land were high; only uncleared land in and beyond the mountains could be had at rational prices, and the plan was soon dropped. So, for one reason or another, were the other enterprises the elder du Pont had in mind.

It was at this point that Irénée du Pont's thoughts turned back to his youthful experience of powdermaking. Here was a process he knew very well. The three ingredients— saltpeter, sulfur and charcoal—were crushed separately, then mixed together in the proportion of 75 to 15 to 10. The mixture was "concentrated" by stamping, then grained or sifted to proper size, dried in the sun. It was "glazed" or polished by being tumbled, then freed of dust by sifting through horsehair netting, and packed into kegs.

American powdermakers during the Revolution had made some acceptable powder although 90 per cent had been bought from France.* By 1800 explosions and British competition had put most of the domestic mills out of business. Du Pont visited the few survivors, found their methods outmoded, and decided that "such competitors should not be formidable." For $36,000, he estimated, he could set up a plant that would earn $10,000 a year.

After discussing the idea with his father, he returned to France to raise capital. He returned with, among other things, the "Articles of Incorporation for the Establishment of a Manufacture of Military and Sporting Powder in the United States of America." These placed the capital of the company at $36,000, in eighteen shares of $2000 each. Three shares had been sold in France, Du Pont de Nemours Père, Fils et Compagnie pledged itself to take eleven, and four were held open for possible American subscribers.

The open shares were soon taken by Archibald McCall, a Philadelphia merchant, and Peter Bauduy, a Frenchman living in Wilmington, Delaware. Irénée was to direct the enterprise for $1800 a year and one-third of the profits or losses. Now all that remained was to find a site, and build.

*French powder was first-rate; Lavoisier had doubled its firing range through his work at the *Régie des Poudres.* But the colonists were disillusioned when a "gift" from the French Government was later billed to them at 20 sols a pound, four times its normal cost.

"AN ASTONISHING AMOUNT OF WORK"

President THOMAS JEFFERSON suggested that the Du Pont mills be located near Washington. But no suitable site could be found; locations examined near Philadelphia, near Paterson in New Jersey, and on the Hudson River also proved unsatisfactory. At last, near Wilmington, du Pont found what he wanted. On the Brandywine Creek was the site of what had been the first cotton mill in America. The mill had burned down, but a dam was available and a few outbuildings and roads remained. Du Pont bought, for $6740, ninety-five acres of land fronting on the stream.

He arrived on the ground on July 19, 1802, assembled men like David Murphy, and began building to the specifications shown on these pages. (David Murphy went on the Du Pont payroll in 1802 as a construction laborer and remained as an operations worker when the mills were completed. It is a pattern frequently followed to this day.)

In the winter of 1803 du Pont wrote to his father:

"We have accomplished an astonishing amount of work since August. In three months we have built a large house and barn of stone and the greater part of the refinery; we have repaired the water-course and the sawmill in which we prepare the wood for our framework. This month we have still to build three mills and one or two other buildings; to dig a new race for one of the mills; to make the drying place, the magazine, the workmen's quarters."

But by the following winter the mills were in production, and in the spring of 1804 the first Du Pont powder went on public sale.

On a hill overlooking mills, Irénée du Pont built this home for family soon after arrival. Tradition says all stone came from one huge boulder. House is still used as residence.

The Brandywine, at a spot near the mills. Indians called it Wawaset, meaning "Near the Bend." White man's name came from Andren Brantwyn, a Swedish first settler.*

Company's first office building, 30 paces from founder's home, was welcome relief to Mrs. du Pont since visitors, mail and conferences frustrated efforts to keep house clean.

Water power principle is shown in early engraving. Stream turns wheels, which turn shafts to which gears and stamping pistons are attached.

*A more romantic version credits the scuttling of a shipload of Brandewijn, a Dutch gin, near the stream's mouth. An alternate Indian name was the Tancopanican, as noted in a journal published by E. I. du Pont's daughter, Eleuthera, early in Nineteenth Century.

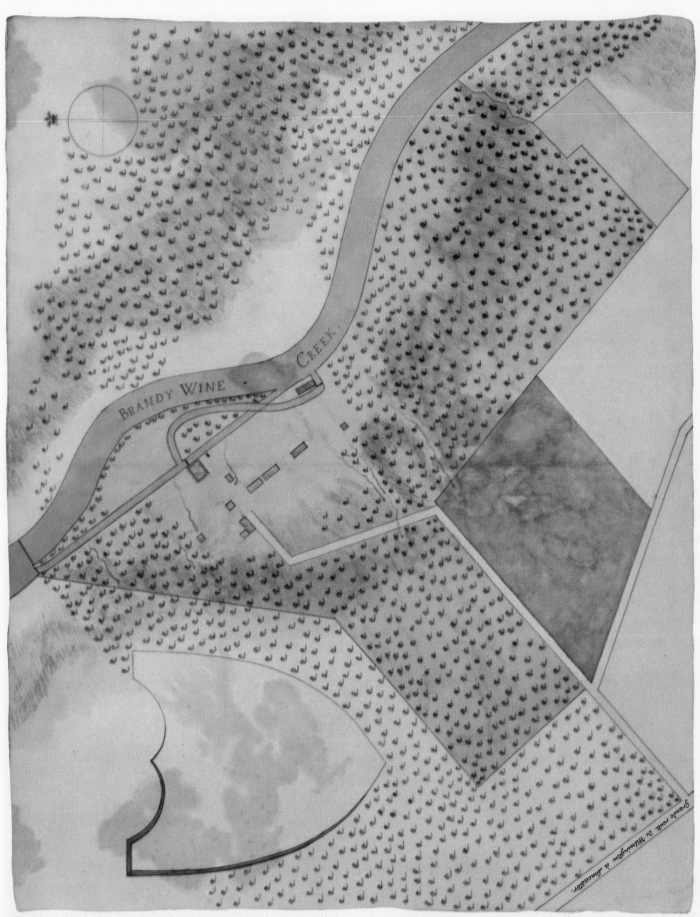

Published here for the first time, this historic document was the initial plan for the mills drawn by Irénée du Pont himself in 1802 after he surveyed the site. Meticulously crayoning a symmetrical forest, he labeled in his native French the "Grande Route" from Wilmington to Lancaster, lower right, and divided the name of the river into two words—Brandy Wine. In construction, he stuck close to his plan for the mill race, center, but changed the location of buildings near the race. The mills were built with three heavy stone walls and one of light wood facing the stream, to minimize explosion hazards. Today, a few vine-covered walls are all that remain of the first mills, which operated for over a century. But, within earshot, other important Du Pont operations still go on.

Antoine Lavoisier, great French chemist, with his wife, painted from life in 1788 by celebrated painter Jacques Louis David. Ironically, David later was member of Revolutionary Convention that sentenced the scientist to death. Copy of painting is in Lavoisier Library at Du Pont Experimental Station. Original is now in Rockefeller Institute.

ROAD TO THE

Painting by Stanley Arthurs shows
Thomas Jefferson, right, urging E. I.
du Pont to go into the powder business.
Paul Revere, second from left, was at
1801 meeting. Jefferson gave du Pont
his first order—refining some saltpeter.

Pierre Samuel du Pont, father of company's founder, painted from life by
Rembrandt Peale. Du Pont lived from
1739 to 1817, is buried near mills. In
France, du Pont was a notable figure.

BRANDYWINE

THE MILLS ON THE BRANDYWINE

First Du Pont mills, built on Brandywine Creek near Wilmington, as painted by John W. McCoy II, who also did paintings at right and on opposite page, top.

First office building was built in 1817 on site near the first mills. It remained in use until last years of the century. Building still stands, in good repair.

Mills in 1840, a contemporary painting by Bass Otis, show little change from early structures. Life still was pastoral and workers' wives strolled around freely.

"Eleutherian Mills," spread along Brandywine in 1806, included grazing land for horses and imported Merino sheep.

Artist McCoy did much research at site on picture, which was presented to Pierre S. du Pont on his 80th birthday.

Howard Pyle's painting shows guarded powder wagons on trip to front in War of 1812. Actually, safety practice forbade wagons traveling this close together.

Financial panics plagued country and company. First nation-wide depression ruined many customers who failed owing money to Du Pont Co.

The question of rights to water from the Brandywine harassed E. I. du Pont. A contemporary cartoon shows him carrying Father Neptune along the creek while a former property owner begs for water. Charge was unfair: firm had already granted rights.

DOUBTS AND DEBTS

Slow mails also handicapped du Pont. Desperately needing cash to meet bank notes, he often waited months for his payments.

"I HAVE spent my life here," Irénée du Pont wrote to a friend in France, "building up a very difficult industry, and the disappointments I have had to bear have given me an habitual dullness and melancholy . . . I owe more than sixty thousand dollars, chiefly in notes at the banks, so that my debts amount to far more than my profits from the powder. The signatures that must be renewed every 60 days put me in exactly the situation of a prisoner on parole who must show himself to the police every month."

Du Pont's main problem all through his 32 years on the Brandywine was shortage of liquid capital. This was partly the fault of his original investors. Though they had promised funds to build and run the mills, only a part had been paid; the difference had to be raised through notes. When the mills began to make money, stockholders insisted he periodically pay out all earnings in dividends, instead of plowing back a portion to increase production and sales. His investors were thinking in 18th Century terms; he was thinking as businessmen do in the 20th Century. His way out of the impasse was to purchase their stock. They demanded tremendous prices — he signed more notes to meet them.

"It is cruel," he once wrote, "to ride 60 miles every five or six days to meet one's notes, and so to waste one's time and one's life. God grant that some day I may get to the end of it."

But he never quite did; and there must have been times when he envied David Murphy, whose work and worries were over at sundown.

The human side of his struggle lives in his letters of the early years. Once, when his brother was ill, he was absent for a time and the mills were left in his wife's charge. Her husband advised her by mail, though making it clear that she was to exercise her best judgment.

"The door of the small furnace is almost out of service," he warned. "Have it repaired . . . at least so that it can be used once more. Take good care of the drying of the powders, and . . . remember, if you please, to glaze the FFr* almost not at all and especially not to glaze the FFg or Rifle when they are too damp.

"I embrace you with all my heart," he concluded, but as a practical postscript added: "If you have need to send powder to New Castle, hire two horses from the neighbors to put to ours."

Modern housewives may well reflect upon young Mrs. du Pont, glazing and delivering gunpowder between household chores and the care of a brood of young children.

One day in March, 1818, tragedy struck. Despite all precautions, an ex-

*F is the measure of the fineness of black powder, then as now. F's run up to seven; the more F's the finer the powder.

Old print shows camp of dragoon troop which guarded mills from enemy attack in War of 1812. Powder was rushed to Lewes, eighty miles distant, to repel British squadron invading Delaware Bay.

Stone masons were among first employees of the Du Pont Company, fashioned the walls of the early mills. From the beginning, the firm did its own construction. Practice is still followed today.

plosion wrecked much of the works, killing forty men.* Neither the laws nor the customs of those days committed the company to take notice of the plight of the widows and orphans. But du Pont pensioned the widows and gave them houses to live in, and undertook the education and medical care of the orphans. There was no full treasury to disburse funds; du Pont paid the cost by renewing his notes and signing more. The plant was rebuilt by the same means; the "prisoner on parole," refusing to be crushed by misfortune, had extended his own sentence by mortgaging the future.

An account of Du Pont operating procedures was given by a Baron Klinckowstrom, a Swedish ordnance expert, who visited the mills in 1819. In a report to the King, he tells of the methods used and of Du Pont's "arrangements" or inventions. One, an early labor-saving device, was a large circular plane fitted with sieves for kerneling powder. The Baron reported approvingly that "water power gives to this plane the same motion as when a man stands at a sieve and swings it back and forth."

The visitor was impressed with Du Pont's careful attention to raw material preparation. Charcoal was made from willow trees "of which, since the tree always grows new branches, they have an inexhaustible

supply." The saltpeter was, he noted, put through a thorough cleaning "no matter how clean and strong when received" and the sulfur was "pure and in color very pretty and clear."

Thus early, it was recognized that quality was a matter of pride, with which no compromise could be made. In 1819 a newspaper as far away as Boston, writing about gunpowder manufacture on the Brandywine, remarked with some astonishment:

"Proposals have been several times

WIDOWS AND ORPHANS

July, 1819—Credit to the account $600.00
March, 1820—Debit to the account 600.00
(detail below)

Deposit of $600 sent from Philadelphia for the relief of the sufferers at the explosion of Eleutherian Mills the 19 March 1818 as follows—which sums are passed to their respective credits Petit Ledger.

Widow Bradley	4 children	$105.00
Widow Gallagher	2 "	55.00
Widow Bready	2 "	55.00
Widow Reynolds	4 "	105.00
Widow Finigan	2 "	50.00
Clo Bready	3 "	80.00
Tenners	3 "	100.00
P. Quigg		30.00
Hugh Sineh		20.00
		$600.00

Widows of explosion victims were pensioned for life by du Pont. Disbursements are shown here as entered on old ledger page.

made to Messrs. Du Pont to manufacture inferior powder for shipping, and to sell it, under the sanction of their name, at a little less price. They have constantly refused."

Dubious opportunities to turn a quick profit received a sharp answer. Once, when the company treasury was especially low, du Pont was offered a premium price, in spot cash, for a large order of cannon and musket powder. One of the States of the Union, irritated at a new Federal tariff law, had threatened to resist enforcement by force of arms. Du Pont replied that he had no powder for such a purpose.

The death of his brother in 1828, and of his wife in 1829, left du Pont to carry on his lifelong struggle with debt without the affection and emotional support he had always drawn from them. He found his only relief in his younger children.

Nonetheless, he was encouraged at signs of a growing American industry. "Manufacturing," he noted, "is a true creation of wealth. It is taking cotton which costs 20 cents per pound and making it *worth* several dollars." It was a prophetic analysis of things to come.

He died in 1834, worn and tired at 63. But he had not struggled in vain. Du Pont powder was selling well all over the country and as far away as South America. And almost all the notes had, with great travail, been paid.

*Miss Betsy Montgomery, a gossipy Wilmington lady who wrote a book of reminiscences, reported that she was at Second and King Streets when the blast occurred, a good six miles from the mills, and was "thrown into a panic" by the shock.

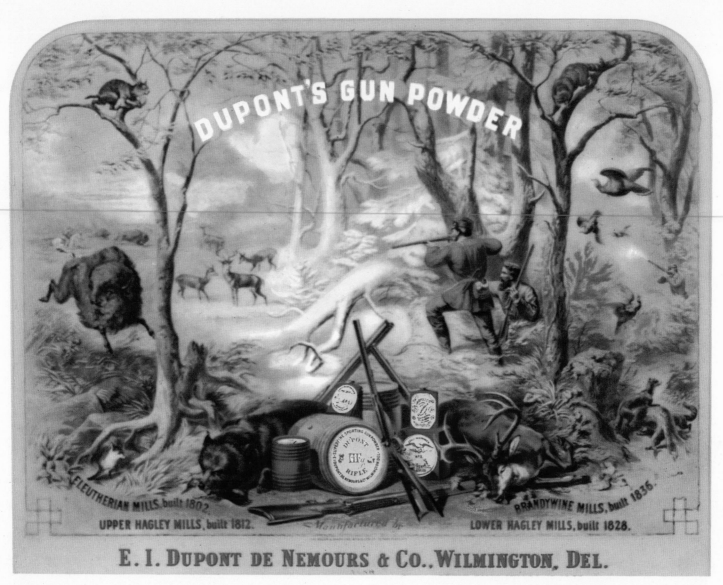

Advertising posters such as this indicate the importance of gunpowder to a nation abounding in game. Du Pont posters became familiar 19th Century decorations on walls of stores where powder was sold. Copy was as colorful as the scenes depicted.*

Powder flasks and canisters were as necessary to settlers as food and drink. Many of these containers are individually owned and highly prized.

Powder keg, made at the mill, held 25 pounds, was a common sight in dealers' stores across the new country.

20

*One ad, for Du Pont's Eagle-brand powder, read: "From foaming Brandywine's rough shores it came to sportsmen dear, its merits and its name: Du Pont's best Eagle, matchless for its power. Strong, swift and fatal, as the bird it bore."

THE SEEDLING TAKES ROOT

NEITHER financial worries nor resistance by investors could swerve Eleuthère Irénée du Pont from his curiously modern idea of how a company could best make its way in the world. In good times and bad, he sought means to increase the quality of his product and improve his methods—the familiar product-and-process-improvement approach of present-day industry. Nor could the pleas of some stockholders keep him from insistence on lowering prices through expanded output. He even anticipated, in a limited way, the modern device of enlarging a company's income and usefulness by what is now called "diversification." He sold refined saltpeter, creosote and "iron liquor" for use in the dyeing of leather and calico.

There were few years in which his output of gunpowder did not increase. In 1804, the first year of production, he made 44,907 pounds and sold them for $15,116.75. Sales in 1805 came to just over three times as much. In 1808, an additional mill and other facilities brought annual production to 300,000 pounds. In 1810, profits exceeded $30,000; in 1811 they approached $45,000. By 1811, too, the Du Pont mills were the largest on this side of the Atlantic. Although there were at the time no railroads and few canals, and many roads were all but impassable, Du Pont powder managed to get where it was needed. Coastal schooners carried it north to Boston, south to Charleston and Savannah; local agents distributed it from those points. Wagon

People had to live near their jobs in early days. Substantial houses like these were built for powder workers.

teams also fanned out from Wilmington, carrying it directly to customers. At the mills, grain for the horses was grown in nearby fields—an early example of industrial integration.

The War of 1812 brought Government orders totaling 750,000 pounds of gunpowder. This looked like a profitable assignment, but the business realities proved otherwise. The company had to risk every dollar of its cash and borrow heavily to extend the capacity of the mills. An adjoining property, known as the Hagley Estate, was purchased. Here additional facilities were erected, to be known as the Hagley Yards—the first major expansion in the company's history.

For David Murphy, employment with Du Pont solved his immediate problem, and it was to provide him with a way of life well suited to his talents. He enjoyed stable working conditions (it has not been unusual for generations of a family to remain in the company's employ) and rates of pay that permitted him to rear his family in comfort. Best of all, he was to work with his employer in an atmosphere of mutual respect and regard.

By 1827, Du Pont employed 140 men, their homes dotting the creek-bank, the gay cries of their children echoing through the woods. In 1834, the output of the corps of workmen, with constantly improving machinery and equipment, exceeded 1,000,000 pounds. The mills on the Brandywine had become a major American business enterprise.

E. I. DU PONT DE NEMOURS & COMPANY
(Co-Partnership)

OPERATING INVESTMENT

DECEMBER 31, 1809

Cash		$ 1,911.66	2%
Accounts and Notes Receivable		33,044.11	30
Inventories		25,808.98	24
Gun powder made and in fabrication	$ 3,272.64		
Gun powder in hands of Agents	18,508.00		
Cooperage	321.00		
Saltpetre	2,938.71		
Brimstone	336.63		
Charcoal wood	432.00		
Plants and Properties		42,750.00	39
Miscellaneous Securities		5,712.97	5
Total Operating Investment		$109,227.72	100%

First formal financial reckoning of the company's fiscal position was made in 1809, seven years after the business had been formed.

E. I. DU PONT DE NEMOURS & COMPANY
(Co-Partnership)

OPERATING INVESTMENT

OCTOBER 31, 1834

Cash		$ 6,902.67	2%
Accounts and Notes Receivable		78,363.42	25
Inventories		66,928.18	21
Gun powder made and in fabrication	$ 6,933.04		
Gun powder in hands of Agents	21,083.00		
Empty Casks	525.18		
Stone, Coal	175.50		
Live Stock, Farming Utensils, etc.	3,770.00		
Saltpetre	29,094.75		
Brimstone	1,443.30		
Charcoal wood	3,903.41		
Plants and Properties		162,850.00	51
Miscellaneous Securities		2,080.00	1
Total Operating Investment		$317,124.27	100%

Company's operating investment on day of founder's death reveals growth and expansion that took place during E. I. du Pont's life.

EPILOGUE

The Legacy of Eleuthère Irénée du Pont

With this office desk and chair, Eleuthère Irénée du Pont began his career in the United States. Head of firm used them until 1900.

ELEUTHÈRE IRÉNÉE DU PONT did more than create a family business. He bred also a tradition, as sturdy and enduring as the stone walls and buttresses of his early mills. It has been said that every precept that guides the Du Pont Company today stems from the rich soil of the Brandywine Valley.

Eleuthère Irénée du Pont antedated his century both in technical and social consciousness. "No privilege exists," his father once told him, "that is not inseparably bound to a duty." It was a theme that characterized his entire life; it is a principle that was to be ingrained deeply into the being of the company that bears his name.

The sense of duty showed early when he pledged his fortune to care for the survivors of the explosion that leveled the mills. Eleuthère Irénée du Pont assumed simply that the privilege of being an employer brought with it an obligation to his employees. It was the same sense of duty that led him to build his own home adjacent to the powder yard. If he asked others to risk their lives, then he and his family would share that danger. Down through the generations, more than one du Pont was to die in deference to that principle.

Eleuthère Irénée du Pont had, too, a sense of obligation to his customers rare in the business world of his time. Again and again he was to stake his personal fortunes on fulfillment of his word. Quality he guarded zealously. Once, during a powder shortage, floor sweepings from other mills were selling at six to eight dollars a keg; du Pont needed money desperately, but would not allow a pound of inferior powder to leave the yards.

When du Pont came to the Brandywine in 1802, it was as a man strange in dress, manner and language, from a nation then unpopular with Americans. But at his death in 1834, Wilmington read in its newspaper: "No event within our recollection has spread a deeper gloom over this community than the sudden death of this excellent man. . . . We have lost a friend whom we loved and venerated, this community a benefactor — our State its most useful and valuable citizen."

Eleuthère Irénée du Pont lived by a code of business honor indistinguishable from his code of personal integrity. Along the Brandywine today, the granite of the old walls tells its own story. The mills have long since been replaced by more efficient, more elaborate structures, and more modern products. But the stone, like the spirit and example of the builder, remains — proud, unshaken and imperishable.

AMERICA
ON THE MARCH
1834-1860

Tracks of wagon trains, still discernible, traced America's most thrilling history. Threading westward in constant streams, they crossed Rockies and pushed on. Du Pont had agent at Independence, Mo., marshaling point, and Du Pont powder rode in nearly every train.

Mill dams marked route of settlers as they made their way west. Soon, many swift-running streams beyond the Alleghenies were dammed.

Whale oil, for home lighting, was an expensive luxury, but the demand for it was so great that America's whaling fleet numbered 680 ships. It roamed the world to fill the growing U. S. need.

THE YOUNG NATION

Messrs. Currier & Ives Relate

BOTH Benjamin Franklin and Thomas Jefferson were enthusiastic prophets of national expansion. Both felt, however, that it would take generations, perhaps centuries, to settle the 3,000,000 square miles of wilderness that was the America of that day.

Both were wrong, and for reasons which both, as inventive men, might have foreseen. In the year of Franklin's death, James Watt invented the steam engine. Five years after Jefferson's end, the engine had been mounted on a carriage and was hauling the nation's freight on rails.

Sight and sound of railway train excited travel-minded U. S. By 1860, "steam cars" of 463 railroads chugged over 30,635 miles of track. Rails carried goods west, brought back grain, ore, cattle. Farms developed along lines. Army found it cheaper to ride rails than to march.

World's first railway suspension bridge, considered "the dream of a madman," was opened to the public and spanned Niagara River in

They were early sources of power for industry and reservoirs for dry seasons. Settlements stuck close to water power across the nation.

Steamboat whistles could be heard on U. S. rivers by 1855. Before Civil War more than 5000 vessels were plying waterways, adding new, rich chapters to U. S. legend. Boats speeded the fast-growing nation's commerce and united the country but often blew up at the wharf.

BULGES ITS BORDERS

the Story of America's Growth

Within half a century, a hundred and fifty thousand miles of track were to web the nation. Du Pont powder blasted rights of way through mountains, gulches and gullies, and behind the shining rails came population.

In a small shop in New York City, a lithographer named Nathaniel Currier and his brother-in-law, James Ives, recorded the great expansion in hundreds of colored prints that were to pass into the folklore of the nation. Some of their pictorial impressions of this expansive era, curiously akin to modern "picture journalism," are noted here.

Game was needed desperately and the herds of bison which roamed western plains proved an easy source of food. Beef cattle were scarce; the bison were slaughtered at an astounding rate.

1855. Bridging the dangerous gorge, it had two levels; upper carried three sets of railroad tracks, the lower had one lane for carriages.

Forests gave way to land-hungry settlers who left what they considered "the overcrowded East" to build their homes in the wilderness. These pioneers used Du Pont powder to clear farms, hunt game. Deere's steel plow (1837) opened bottom lands too wet for earlier plows.

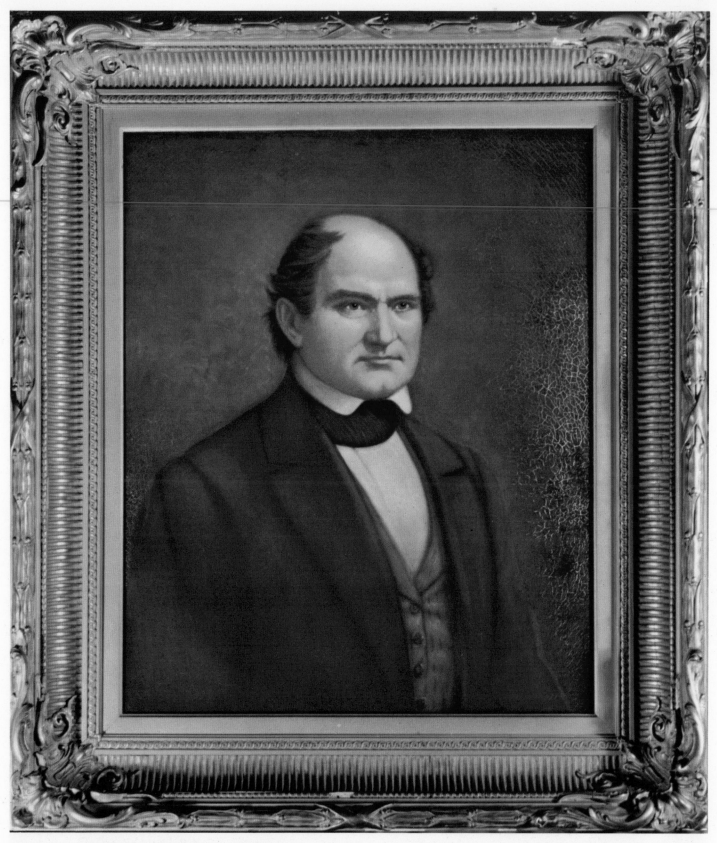

ALFRED VICTOR DU PONT

Alfred Victor du Pont, eldest son of the founder, came to the Brandywine as a four year old child, and literally grew up in the mills. After his father's death in 1834, he became senior partner. A scientist and inventor, he was happier when designing machinery and experimenting with chemicals than in conducting business affairs. Yet, during his regime the company flourished and helped the U. S. win the Mexican War. In 1850 he retired, and died six years later — still within sound of the pulsing powder yards.

HENRY DU PONT

Second son of the founder, Henry du Pont became head of the firm in 1850, and until his death in 1889, on his 77th birthday, he devoted each waking moment to the company's affairs. As senior partner, he inherited large debts but a growing business, and he made it the best known explosives company in the nation. An ardent Whig, he admired Henry Clay and so named a settlement of workers' houses near the mills. He wore a high hat on all occasions, once used it to scoop water from a race to put out a fire.

HENRY DU PONT
1850 — 1889

27

INVENTORS GO TO WORK

THROUGHOUT history, invention has flourished only when men were free and channels of communication open. The new American nation thus provided precisely the climate in which technology can best be nurtured and developed.

Among the founders themselves were some, like Franklin and Paine,* who were notable inventors. Perhaps it was this that led the Constitution to provide that the innovator should, for a period of time, be granted the exclusive rights to original discoveries.

The outburst of human energy that followed was unlike anything yet to appear on earth. So many inventions were filed that in 1832 the director of the Patent Bureau wailed that no more fields remained unconquered!

Despite the rush of original ideas, the great American contribution lay not in scientific abstraction but in organizing invention to mass production ends. Initiative was spurred on apace. Everywhere, men were at work on new things. As reported in the pictorial press of the day—a robust journalism that covered all phases of life—they were succeeding. They perceived even then that in this simple course lay the way to profit, and to progress. And the spirit of the times was nowhere more apparent than in the stone mills that bordered the tumbling Brandywine.

Samuel Morse invented telegraph in 1832, became familiar sight in the day's pictorial press. Telegraph poles went west with the railroads, sliced weeks from communications.

Cyrus Hall McCormick's reaper, developed in 1833 and improved in following years, replaced the scythe for cutting grain. In 1830, the human labor factor needed to produce one bushel of grain was three and a half hours. Sixty years later, it was but 10 minutes.

28

*Irénée du Pont was interested, but must have been skeptical of one plan. Paine had proposed to propel a vehicle by the successive explosions of minute quantities of gunpowder, each turning a shaft through the thrust of a piston. Though the fuel was different, and perhaps impractical, Paine's idea was, of course, a precursor of the modern internal combustion engine.

Improved methods of weaving increased textile production, removed spinning and weaving of cloth from the housewife's chores. Women's suffrage owes debt to such industrial time-savers as this.

Gaslight, long a source of street illumination, now entered the home. Supply failures were common and candles were kept close by. Despite this, it was a great improvement over earlier methods.

The transatlantic cable, developed by Cyrus Field in 1858, ended America's insularity, forecast its place as a world power. Cable broke shortly after it was laid, but was repaired in 1866.

The sewing machine, invented by Elias Howe in 1845, eased women's tasks and offered them increased leisure time. Used immediately by textile industry, it brought in ready-to-wear clothing.

Four Inventors Were Honored on U.S. Postage

Eli Whitney's cotton gin fathered the U. S. textile industry.*

Cyrus McCormick's improved reaper was farmer's best friend.

Elias Howe's sewing machine did great things for housewife.

Samuel Morse's telegraph sped communication in growing U.S.

*Whitney's early work was conducted in collaboration with Eliphalet Remington, a gun maker in Ilion, N.Y. Remington Co. in 1933 became a Du Pont affiliate, still makes firearms.

ADAMS-SON

In 1854, the mills on the Brandywine still resembled the earlier buildings, but their number increased and they now strung below and across stream from original mill site. Water was still source of power, but huge pulleys, center and opposite page, supplied it to those

Evaporating kettle, used in the early manufacture of Du Pont powder, is cast-iron, seven feet in diameter, now stands near Brandywine.

THE MILLS IN MID-CENTURY

INSATIABLE, the growing nation called for powder and more powder. Production on the Brandywine expanded even beyond the million-pound-a-year mark. In 1846 the mills took in stride the demands made on them by the Mexican War. Organized mining for gold and silver that followed the gold rush of '49 called for volume production. A mill near Wilkes-Barre was bought and rebuilt to fill demands of booming coal fields.

By no means did Du Pont have the field to itself. Over 200 mills sprang up, in 16 states, many of them managed by able men who pressed the Brandywine mills to new standards of performance. Indeed, it was an industry in which only the competent could, literally, survive.

Du Pont, however, maintained its position with successive improvements.* Already it had learned that leadership was an elusive prize, never won cheaply. At the time the poet Browning was writing "A man's reach should exceed his grasp, or what's a heaven for?" On the Brandywine, Du Pont men went on reaching.

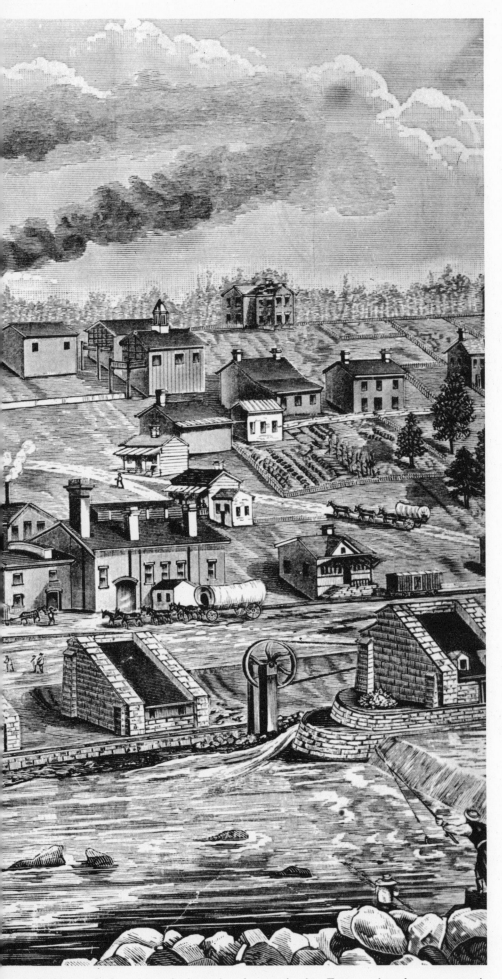

new buildings which could not be located at the water's edge. Trains and tracks were now evident, lower left and far right, but cars were horse-drawn to eliminate danger of flying cinders.

Early research tool was this éprouvette, used to test Du Pont powder. Flight of ball was measured against powder needed to propel it.

*Inventors in other fields were founding new companies that later were to develop into great businesses. Among them: Charles Goodyear, whose discovery of a way to vulcanize rubber was epochal; Gail Borden, who evaporated milk; George Westinghouse, father of the air-brake.

NEW IDEAS

ON the Brandywine, in the early 1850's, a young man not long out of college was dissatisfied with what he found in the yards. He was Lammot du Pont, recently graduated as a chemist from the University of Pennsylvania. In the years to come hundreds of youthful scientists were to follow the path he defined, and for the same reason. Dissatisfaction with existing conditions has been American chemistry's most stimulating quality.

Lammot du Pont, setting up a crude laboratory in an old refinery building, had ideas for improvement which he hoped to effect through chemical research. Like his grandfather, he had a fine sense of the scientific approach, but he never lost sight of economic necessities. His contributions were to prove a rare combination of both.

The urge to do things better had prevailed on the Brandywine from the start. Irénée du Pont had set up his mills on the French pattern, because he thought it superior to the methods then in use in America. But from the beginning he modified, refined and improved. His business outlook was curiously American and curiously modern. The persistent aim was to make his product better and at lower cost, pass the savings on to customers—and so get more people in the habit of using his wares.

Alfred du Pont, too, had introduced many a powdermaking innovation. Continuous production, secret of low cost in so many modern industries,

Lammot du Pont bridged past and present in company history. As a child he brightened declining years of the founder; three of his sons, all living in 1952, served as president.

Early Du Pont research was conducted by Lammot du Pont in building at far left, the old saltpeter refinery on Brandywine. Sons, Pierre S. and Lammot, also worked here.

Coal mines were first users of new powder, which company pioneered in 1850's.

ON AN OLD THEME

was introduced years before the Civil War. The mills worked on shifts around the clock, the night shift eerie with the flicker of lanterns which, then as now, were kept outside and cast their light in through the doorways. Equipment was continually being examined for better performance and efficiency.

When Alfred du Pont assumed command, he designed new kegs for shipping, and set up his own cooperage to make them. The kegs available at the time were poorly made — so poorly in fact that repairs had for years been a spare-time job for powdermen's wives, including those of the du Ponts. The new standardized kegs (pronounced "kags") were stronger, cheaper and more nearly moisture-proof, and provided a distinctive package that increased sales.*

Manufacturing improvements and more efficient methods are elements within the control of the producer. Raw materials frequently are not. It was, therefore, to this phase that Lammot du Pont addressed himself.

Powder as then made required charcoal, sulfur and, importantly, saltpeter, a white crystalline substance which when refined is almost pure potassium nitrate. Charcoal, of course, represented no problem. The grade needed for gunpowder came from willow wood, in which the valley abounded. (Brandywine youngsters early learned to weave the discarded twigs and shoots into basketware.) A "coal house" at the mills did the necessary burning.

Sulfur or "brimstone" was largely imported at the time, mostly from France and Sicily, but it was cheap and relatively plentiful.

But saltpeter, which was anywhere from two-thirds to three-fourths the content of black powder, was another

UNITED STATES PATENT OFFICE.

LAMMOT DU PONT, OF WILMINGTON, DELAWARE.

IMPROVEMENT IN GUNPOWDER.

Du Pont patent substituted abundant sodium nitrate for costly potassium nitrate.

story. The residue of organic decay, it existed in few parts of the world. For three centuries, the soil in parts of India which combined dense population and a dry climate were the primary source. The price fluctuated madly and supply could be and was controlled by blockade, war or emergency. Small quantities could be obtained from caves, deposited there by generations of bats, but it was scarce. For years, Du Pont's most worrisome supply problem had been to insure itself a stockpile of this strategic material.

But on South America's west coast was an area where once dwelt millions of pelicans, cormorants and gannets, all fish-eating birds. Droppings accumulated over the centuries, and no rains came to wash away the salts. In time, nature produced a vast shelf of soft stone that was a form of saltpeter called sodium nitrate. As a component of powder it had limitations; it contained impurities hard to remove. Powder made from it soon became damp and refused to fire.

Lammot du Pont found the way to overcome this deficiency. He devised methods for treating sodium nitrate which made it superior to existing materials, and at a lower cost. The new explosive was called "B blasting powder" or "soda powder." Patented in 1857, it swept the coal and iron fields almost overnight. Soon it had supplanted black powder made with India saltpeter in most blasting.

The new powder represented the first notable change in the composition of black powder in six or seven centuries. But more importantly, it was a step toward national self-sufficiency — a step that was to know many a Du Pont tread in the future. The dream of Irénée du Pont of a self-contained nation was a trifle nearer. But now, for four years, progress was to be deferred. The nation was at war.

Long sea voyage by clipper ships brought India saltpeter to U. S. Du Pont's use of Peruvian (later Chilean) product reduced costs.

Quarries were the immediate beneficiaries of Du Pont discovery. With a more powerful and cheaper powder, their business thrived.

*Let no one underestimate the importance of shipping containers. Today they represent, in dollar volume, one of the company's largest annual purchases.

CIVIL
WAR

DU PONT CANNON HOUSE

THE Civil War transformed the mills on the Brandywine literally into an armed camp. Tradition and sentiment in Delaware inclined it toward the South.* Secession was averted by the narrowest of margins, and many residents were Confederate sympathizers and supporters.

The Du Pont mills, however, were again placed at the disposal of the Federal Government. As the Union's most reliable source of supply their safety became an important project. The premises were guarded day and night. Two companies of workmen were mobilized as volunteer militia to patrol the area. An unusual number of explosions and fires were attributed to enemy sabotage, but no major elements were destroyed. Day and night, the mills devoted themselves to supplying gunpowder while civilian work stopped. It is notable that the shift to military production was purely voluntary, for total war, in the North, at least, was a concept yet to come. A company did war work or not, as it chose, just as draftees often hired substitutes.

Aside from large-scale production, Du Pont made two other contributions that had much to do with the outcome of the war. Working with the Army's Ordnance Department, it finished the development and produced for the first time a special "Mammoth Powder" that made feasible the firing of the heavy artillery that was to revolutionize warfare. And Lammot du Pont, hastily dispatched to England, persuaded the British to rescind their embargo on India saltpeter that threatened to silence every Northern gun. Failure, on any count, might well have rewritten history.

In 1863, Confederate cavalry attacked Gunpowder Bridge, near Baltimore, a vital point on the railway between mills and the front. Two companies of Du Pont men helped repel the attack and keep lines open.

LESLIE'S ILLUSTRATED WEEKLY

*There were no slaves on the Brandywine, but Delaware was a slave state and they were fairly prevalent in the southern counties.

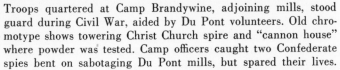

RE BATTERY   CHRIST CHURCH

Powder leaving Du Pont mills during Civil War was shipped on rails of the Philadelphia and Baltimore Central Railroad.* This fine photograph was taken in 1865 at Chadds Ford, Pa., a few miles up the Brandywine from the mills.

Troops quartered at Camp Brandywine, adjoining mills, stood guard during Civil War, aided by Du Pont volunteers. Old chromotype shows towering Christ Church spire and "cannon house" where powder was tested. Camp officers caught two Confederate spies bent on sabotaging Du Pont mills, but spared their lives.

The Rodman gun was largest of its kind at time of Civil War. Except at short range these guns burst at the breech when fired. Rodman, the inventor, turned to Lammot du Pont, who helped develop "Mammoth Powder," with grains up to the size of baseballs. This slowed the rate of burning and propelled, rather than blasted, greatly increasing the big gun's range of fire.

BRADY PHOTO FROM U. S. SIGNAL CORPS.

*A connecting spur was built from Montchanin, near the yards, during the Civil War. Link to through railway was essential, as "off the railroad" mills were at a serious disadvantage. Shipment by Conestoga wagons continued, however, until 1880's, as powder wasn't welcomed on rails.

NATIONAL
SECURITY

THE Civil War, like all wars, past and present, was a severe blow to the nation and to business enterprise. It was no less so to Du Pont. Explosives sold for military purposes create neither markets nor wealth. The costs of war are borne by the entire economy, and taxation, dislocation and interruption of normal progress exact a high price.

That had been true as early as the War of 1812, when the company had felt obliged to ignore "civilian" production to supply the American Army and Navy. It netted far less money than it could have made by supplying the incessant demands for hunting and blasting powders—and it was many years getting back the markets it had surrendered to others.

Much the same thing happened in the Civil War, except that the financial blow was many times more severe. Agents in the Southern states, with inventories unpaid for, had to be written off. Promising developments had to be deferred. The new "soda powder" was just then sweeping the mining and construction industries, and it was a disappointment to relinquish the field to companies that sprang up overnight to capitalize on the need. But Henry du Pont, in accepting the situation, felt that the company was performing nothing more than a simple duty.

During the Civil War, Du Pont produced for the Army and Navy an average of a million pounds of powder a year, and sold it under the public market price. Henry du Pont viewed this wartime record with vast personal and company pride. Never, he pointed out, had a nation at war had its powder so cheaply.

With the inevitability of fate, Du Pont found itself and its employees attacked after the war in the day's version of "Merchant of Death" charges. This both puzzled and angered the head of the firm and his workmen. Neither he nor they were to be the last Du Pont people to undergo this sad experience, and to be similarly puzzled and distressed.

One of earliest photographs of the mills, apparently made from old glass plate negative, shows section of Brandywine yards and Henry Clay dam as they appeared during war.

INDUSTRIAL
EXPANSION
1865-1902

One of world's great news pictures was taken when East and West were linked by steel rails, joined by a golden spike. Historic meeting of roads, pushing from both East and West, took place at Promontory Point, Utah, on May 10, 1869, as railway workers cheered.

New farm machines boosted food output as Midwest became U. S. breadbasket. In colonial days, 19 farmers clothed and fed themselves and one city person. By 1880 same number supplied 132.

Meat became plentiful with development of barbed wire to keep cattle from wandering and refrigerated railroad cars to rush meat to markets. Cattle population almost doubled from 1875-1890.

A NEW TIDE OF EXPANSION

Explosives helped dig ore from mines. Mine name, "Neversweat," shown in rare photo, also was given masons by early powdermen.

Steel mills needed explosives to blast limestone for flux. Steel production jumped from 13,000 tons in 1860 to 4,790,320 in 1890.

LIBRARY OF CONGRESS

Immigrants at Battery Park, N. Y., after trip from Ellis Island, were part of millions of new Americans who came in '80's and '90's.

WITH the Civil War over, America stood free to resume development. And develop it did: in the 35 remaining years of the Nineteenth Century, the country, freed of restraints, underwent an era of growth exceeding that of any period, before or since.

The westward movement was still on; new States entered the Union in batches. In the early 1880's the nation's unity was signaled by the adoption of the "time zones," and the officialization of a "Standard Time" in each. The U. S. A. was growing up.

The frontier was still raw and at times bleeding on the edges and hostile Indians staged sporadic outbreaks; Custer's Last Stand and the misdeeds of the Apache made it plain that progress was not cheaply purchased. But on the whole the winning of the West was as businesslike and productive as it was picturesque and dramatic. By 1869 the first transcontinental railroad was completed and presently most of the country was crisscrossed with railroads. In the 1880's, 65,000 miles of new track were laid, a 10-year record that still stands. Railroads required steel and coal, and those two industries alone were soon producing more wealth than California gold rushers had dreamed possible. In 1860, U. S. industrial production was two thirds that of Great Britain; by 1895 it was to be twice as great!

A new relationship, based on invention,* was developing between industry and agriculture. On the vast prairies, a few men with ingenious new machinery could raise wheat by the hundreds of thousands of bushels. The refrigerator car gave cattlemen markets a thousand miles away. Barbed wire, confining cattle on the treeless plains, cheered ranchers—the animals strayed so far afield they were tough and stringy. Later, plastics were to end the day of the long-horn steer, which had survived because there was a demand for the horn, used for combs, buttons and other needs. (The Doyle Works at Leominster, Mass., now a part of the Du Pont Company, was a large user before converting to plastics.) Henceforth, the emphasis would be on beef.

Increasing the supply of goods was a prime need for the expanding nation. Increasing opportunity was another, for with the century's close came the end of the "free land" offered in the Homestead Acts of 1862. And population was mounting. In 1800, when E. I. du Pont arrived in the country, population stood at 5 million; in 1900, it reached 76 million. Many were Europeans who had come, as he had, to share in the nation's development. In his day, political freedom had started the nation on its path as a land of promise. Industrial development, now spreading across the growing nation, was bringing the promise true.

*Dramatic evidence of how freedom and incentive furthered development may be seen in the rise in the *number* of inventions regarded as "significant." Starting with 7 in the Eleventh Century, the list grows very slowly: in the Fourteenth Century there were 30 and in the Seventeenth, 42. But in the Nineteenth, when individual initiative was finding full flower, there were 197!

Spire of Christ Church, center, overlooks the valley scene. Powdermen's homes, clustered in groups known as "banks," lined the
stream, as a housewife's well-filled washline, lower left, attests.
Here we look north from Breck's Mill dam, below Hagley Yards.

BRANDYWINE HEYDAY:

Du Pont people lived, worked and played together in Eighties with
little outside contact. Typical social occasion was church picnic
like this from Greenhill Presbyterian. Many of these powdermen
and their families had been in company's employ for generations.

Powdermen and families dressed up on Sunday to attend one of the four churches in area. Here are the H. Greens, of Henry Clay.

Hagley Yard foreman, John Stewart, occupied a slate-roofed* house. Married men got rent-free houses, bachelors boarded out.

First Du Pont Photographer Chronicles an Era

IN the 1880's, a Du Pont employee named Pierre Gentieu appeared at the mills one day with a camera, then a rarity among amateurs. His pictures were in great demand, and he roamed the yards, recording a way of life that by his time had reached its heyday. The sylvan settings of the valley were becoming as outmoded as the water power of the mills, for newer factories used steam power, and steam was cheaper in the cities. Life on the Brandywine, little changed from the pattern of a century earlier, went on unruffled. But the handwriting already was on the walls.

PIERRE GENTIEU

Neighborhood children rejoiced when schoolhouse was turned to collateral duty as polling place. This was election day, 1888.

Powderman's clothing, including boots, was designed to lessen hazards. Children bringing dad's lunch parked shoes at plant gate.

When work was slack at the mills, employees built fences and roads. Here they repair the lower Hagley dam after spring freshet.

*Many houses of Du Pont workmen, as well as other company-owned properties, got slate-shingle roofs when a slate quarry went into bankruptcy and settled its debt to company with carload of slate. Roofs survive to this day on numerous buildings.

Engaging this boy's attention is a stereoscope, through which double-imaged photographs, similar to those on these pages, seemed to take on three dimensions. A favorite pastime of the '90's, it was one way in which people, with more leisure and money, had a good time.

ENTER REFINEMENTS: SACRED AND PROFANE

IN the latter part of the Nineteenth Century, industry's progress was making life more pleasant for a broader cross-section of the population. Especially in the growing cities did new conveniences and luxuries appear to meet popular approval. One fad of the day was the stereoscope, through whose lenses we note here the advance of refinements, sacred and profane, which ranged through all phases of U. S. life.

Rapidly growing cities needed more and faster transportation even before age of suburbs. Tracks were laid and the

That peculiarly American institution, the soda fountain, made its appearance before an appreciative audience at this

Menus of good restaurants began to feature wide variety of fresh foods, made possible through better railroad transportation, refrigerator cars.

This is what they meant by carriage trade in the '80's and '90's. The coach-and-four was impressive in the park,

horse-drawn street car clattered down the rails. Horse population exceeded 35 million in 1900, is now 7 million.

Department stores, really great bazaars under one roof, featured window displays that lured ladies with a new female pastime—window shopping. As people demanded more and better things, a number of small "dry goods emporia" expanded to become today's large department stores.

time, soon became a neighborhood gathering place, took many goodies and luxury delicacies into the popular market.

Kindergarten classes, with scrubbed, preschool children under supervision of primly dressed teachers, swarmed over parks of cities like Richmond, Va., where this pastoral scene was enacted. First popular in the '80's, kindergartens were usually confined at this time to privately run schools.

but for the great mass of people it was strictly a spectator sport. Few city residents owned private transportation.

The bicycle craze swept the nation in the Eighties and Nineties. People rode bicycles for pleasure, to work, for exercise. They became a traffic hazard and, in self-protection, cities were forced to pave streets to prevent injuries. At height of the craze, cigar consumption dropped a million a day.

Repauno, N. J., plant, built in 1880, was brainchild of Lammot du Pont. With his cousin William he used rowboat to cross Dela- ware River daily from Chester, Pa. Contemporary sketch shows units of works, later to become world's largest dynamite plant.

REPAUNO—AND A NEW CHALLENGE

ALFRED NOBEL, a modest and self-effacing Swede, was, oddly enough, to perpetuate his name in many ways. The highest awards for achievement in the sciences, literature and the cause of peace now commemorate his work. So do the developments that grew out of his scientific accomplishments. For these he won no prize, but they earned him the gratitude of man. And they were to have a profound effect upon the Du Pont Company.

Nobel's work was preceded by another discovery that was to have notable reverberations on the Brandywine. In Turin, Italy, Ascanio Sobrero invented a liquid explosive of tremendous power called nitroglycerin. It was so unpredictable that even its discoverer was appalled and frightened, and warned against its use.

But in 1866, Alfred Nobel found that by saturating a porous material with nitroglycerin, he could control the action within safe limits. The explosive, which he called dynamite, was literally to change the face of the earth.

It was the most powerful blasting agent yet known. In a few deafening seconds it could rend and shatter hard rock far beyond the capacity of black powder.

At once quarries, mines and construction projects began calling for dynamite. Henry du Pont was far from convinced that the newcomer would ever replace black powder. But Lammot du Pont saw it as the industry's future. Although it was not a Du Pont invention he saw that here was a chance to make a real contribution to its development through technical and production skill. Who, after all, he asked his associates, knew more about making explosives?

In January of 1880, on the far bank of the Delaware River, a new plant began rising from the frozen earth. Organized with Lammot du Pont as president was a new company to which du Pont, a student of Indian lore, gave the aboriginal name of a small creek near the plant. Within six months of breaking ground, the Repauno Chemical Company was producing 2000 pounds of the new explosive a day, an ambitious production schedule.

Under du Pont's guidance, Repauno developed an able corps of scientists and technicians who were to prove a valuable reservoir of talent. It had its own laboratory where a band of chemists worked shoulder to shoulder with their chief on product-and-process improvement. From this laboratory there issued a steady flow of automatic production techniques that kept raising output, lowering costs, and making production safer.

This was in the ancient company tradition, and so was the way Lammot du Pont lost his life:

Plant wastes were killing shad in the river. A method was devised to recover the harmful acids from nitroglycerin. But one day, in moving up from laboratory to plant scale, something went wrong. Lammot du Pont undertook to prevent impending disaster. Since earliest boyhood, he had staked his life with explosives. This time he lost.

Repauno pioneered measures like wooden walks and rubber-tired buggies that were to lessen hazards of production. Today, only ladies' garment industry has better safety record than explosives.

High explosives burrowed huge tunnels through solid rock to make way for spreading railroads.

Dynamite blasted deep foundations for giants like the Flatiron Building.

New York's subway, opened in 1904, used tons of explosives, eased traffic problem.

...IT'S DYNAMITE!

THE impressive thing about dynamite's American debut was the speed, skill and economy with which it accomplished its appointed tasks. Almost overnight it multiplied the productivity of mines. With black powder the great Comstock lode in Nevada had been producing $15,000,000 in silver bullion a year. Dynamite took over and output more than doubled; silver for tableware became commonplace. Coal tonnage quintupled; iron production quadrupled; copper output multiplied nine times in ten years. Nickel, once precious, now plated everything from toys to revolvers.

Not a pound of cement was made in America until dynamite came along to quarry rock; millions of people were soon introduced to the efficiency and convenience of paved sidewalks and good roads. For the first time men tunneled through mountains. Yet dynamite could be controlled so delicately that sculptors were to use it for rough-shaping monumental projects like that at Mt. Rushmore.

For the first time, the earth's crust was as clay in man's hands. And, as always happens when science and industry combine to expand mankind's soaring horizons, everyone benefited.

Paved streets became a reality after dynamite made cement manufacture possible.

Destruction of Flood Rock, a navigation menace near Hell Gate entrance to Long Island Sound, on Oct. 10, 1885, was "the outstanding submarine blast of the 19th Century." Dynamite played big part. A total of 288,936 pounds of explosives shattered the rock.

This is first photograph made with incandescent light. Edison's invention brought age of electricity, revolutionizing living patterns.

Alexander Graham Bell's telephone, invented in 1876, sped communication even in remote areas, became vital part of U. S. life.

FINDING A FORMULA FOR REFORM

IN the second half of the Nineteenth Century, the wave of technical genius that began with the Revolution rolled into a mighty surge. As one new idea followed another, each transforming behavior patterns, one fact became panorama-plain. Invention and development, rather than the shrill voice of protest, were to be the real architects of social reform. Throughout the century, agitation for the relief of humanity's ills rose in quarters ranging from the Knights of Labor to the Populist firebrands of the 1890's. They sponsored legislation for shorter working hours, women's suffrage, for farm reforms and for an end to child labor. All were worthy objectives, but they were not to be reached by political furore. They were to come, in orderly fashion, through the productive capacity brought into being by invention and industrial development.

At mid-point of the century, the American workman had at his disposal one-half a horsepower of energy from machinery and animals, with machines carrying only 5 per cent of the load. By 1900, he commanded twice as much non-human energy, and machines were furnishing 40 per cent of the work energy — and he had doubled his output of goods. Here indeed was the pattern of the future. It was to diminish his hours of labor by nearly half within another fifty years. It was to keep U. S. children in school instead of in factories, although not long before men believed that the world would starve unless it could enlist the labor of everyone down to the age of four years.*

In the inventor's workshop, and the productive processes of industry, the U. S. was finding its true formula for reform. Other nations had tried to achieve the same ends through political fiat — and failed. America's approach was less spectacular, but it was built to endure.

First successful typewriter, created by Christopher Sholes in 1873, brought women into business, helped spread equal rights doctrine.

Linotype, invented by Mergenthaler, brought modern daily newspaper. Widespread information elevated educational standards.

*Jeremy Bentham, noted British economist, was so convinced. But Robert Owen, a manufacturer turned Socialist, disagreed; in 1834 he sought a child labor statute which would limit the working hours of children under 10 to 10½ hours per day!

"ST. LAWRENCE"—WOOD COOK STOVE.

Wood-burning stoves took cooking out of the fireplace.

Combined Sofa and Bath Tub.
THE COMMON SENSE INVENTION OF THE AGE.

Is Practical, Convenient, Economical, Comfortable, Portable, Complete and Cheap.

In presenting this valuable combination to the public we are supplying a long-felt want, and placing a household necessity within the reach of all. It is not only a handsome and desirable piece of household furniture, but combines with it the best of bathing facilities. A full-sized Bath Tub, with water tank of 18 gallons capacity, the most improved Heating Device and complete Waste Water Attachments.

There is also provided a large rubber apron, that buttons on to the inside of outer edge of Bath Tub, folding over the front and covering the carpet one yard, thereby forming a perfect protection to the upholstery and carpet.

The combination can be upholstered appropriately for any room, and the bath used as satisfactorily as if taken in the most modern of bath-rooms.

For full particulars, as to styles of Upholstering, Prices, etc., address.

This ingenious piece of furniture was not successful.

ZERO Refrigerator,

BEST in the World.

A. M. LESLEY, 605 Sixth Ave., New York.

SEND FOR BOOK.

First ice boxes brought new convenience to housewives.

WHAT SHALL WE SLEEP ON?

The attention of every reader who values "Life, Health, and Happiness" is called to the ANSWER to this important question, as found in the wonderful and beautiful

Woven Wire Mattress.

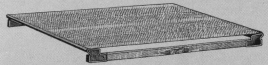

Patented June 16, 1868; Nov. 23 and 30, 1869; Nov. 22, 1870; April 11, 1871.

MANUFACTURED BY THE

Woven Wire Mattress Company of Hartford Ct.

SOLE PATENTEES AND MANUFACTURERS.

For Perfect Cleanliness, Perfect Comfort, and Perfect Durability,

The Company claim that this Perfect Spring Bed without Springs has no rival. The Mattress consists of 8,000 feet of 19½ wire made into perfect coils, and at the same time interlocked by an ingenious process of Double Weaving, by which a fabric half an inch thick is formed, which, when it is stretched on its frame by machinery, forms a bed of remarkable elasticity and strength.

The Wire Mattress is a complete revolution of old ideas as to beds, being a Perfect Sleeping Arrangement in itself, with the addition of a blanket in warm weather. For ordinary use, however, a thin hair mattress is desirable; but this is the only covering necessary, and on this account the bed is the CHEAPEST ARTICLE IN MARKET.

All the vexing repairs usually necessary in almost every other bed are avoided, and they are guaranteed.

NEVER TO LOSE THEIR SHAPE OR NEED A REPAIR.

This wire fabric is as Noiseless as India-Rubber Cloth, which is a strong recommendation to all nervous, restless sleepers. It is destined to be THE POPULAR BED of the country.

Maker claimed mattress never lost its shape or style.

Scientific Suspenders

A much needed Reform.

Perfect Comfort to the Wearer.

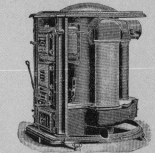

Popular for full dress wear because they cannot crease the shirt bosom and the straps are never seen.

No dragging on the shoulders.

The trousers keep their shape because they are never pulled up from the shoe and there is no strain on the bands. No sewed joints to come apart.

The scientific principle of the pulley acting on the cord insures perfect freedom of movement in any position.

To wear them is to like them.

On sale by all first-class dealers or sent by mail on receipt of price, 50c., $1.00, $1.50 and $2.00, post-paid. State height and weight.

SCIENTIFIC SUSPENDER CO. (Lim.), BUFFALO, N. Y.

Trousers were scientifically secure.

THE NEW MAGEE FURNACE,
THE BOSTON HEATER.

The selection of Heating Apparatus should receive most careful attention. A good furnace is a blessing, but a poor one is a curse.

Send for a descriptive circular of the Magee Furnaces, and read what the users say about their merits. They are the most carefully constructed, the most powerful heaters, and the most economical of any in the market. We warrant them absolutely gas and dust tight, and to give perfect satisfaction in every particular.

MAGEE FURNACE CO.

Nos. 32 to 38 Union, and 19 to 27 Friend Streets, Boston, 92 Beekman St. New-York, 86 Lake St. Chicago, 8 and 10 Pine St. San Francisco.

Central heating brought new comfort.

Indoor plumbing was the period's cardinal advance in personal comfort.

TRIUMPHANT SUCCESS!

THE HOME WASHER!

SAVES Clothes, Labor & Time.

"CLEANLINESS IS AKIN TO GODLINESS."—Benj. Franklin.

Warranted the best Washer Extant,

And the only Machine in the world that washes thoroughly without injury to the fabric.

RETAIL PRICE, WITHOUT WRINGER, $15.

HOME
Manufacturing Comp'y.

PRINCIPAL DEPOTS:

13 Barclay St., near Astor House, New York.
Cor. Clinton & Jackson Sts., Chicago.
818 N. Fourth Street, - - St. Louis.
31 Brattle Street, - - Boston.

SEND FOR CIRCULAR.

Washing machines lightened work.

Holidays are Kodak Days

The long evenings of Christmas-tide are made doubly delightful by taking flash-light pictures of one's friends.

Picture taking by daylight or flash-light is easy with a Kodak.

Kodaks $5.00 to $35.00.

Catalogues free of dealers or by mail.

EASTMAN KODAK CO.

Rochester, N. Y.

Amateurs now could make pictures.

47

NO HELP WANTED

HERE are six lines of commercial activity that find few practitioners today, indispensable as they were in the mid-Eighties, when these pictures were taken. Nostalgic as some of them seem, they represent a phase of U. S. life now succeeded by newer and better ways. This remarkable collection of photographs, some published here for the first time, was discovered recently by the Library of Congress.

The feather-duster salesman and his product, which moved dust from one object to another, lost out to the vacuum cleaner.

The coal man, with his peach basket and push cart, made his departure when motor truck brought coal and fuel oil to doorstep.

The fruit peddler and his unsanitary wares bade an unlamented farewell with advent of modern packaging and merchandising.

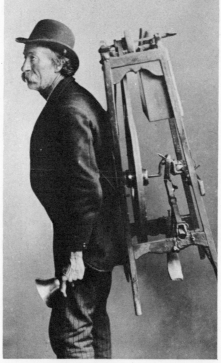

The flypaper and match boy grew up and was never replaced because of screens and air conditioning, pilot lights, electric stoves.

Ambulant scissor-grinder with his loud bell and flashing wheel found work slack when improved metals went into kitchenware.

Consumption of ice quadrupled in last 50 years of 19th Century, but iceman was to become a rarity with new refrigeration.

EUGENE DU PONT
1849 — 1902

EUGENE DU PONT

Eugene du Pont, a grandson of the founder, succeeded his uncle, Henry du Pont, as head of the company. He continued the practice of personally handling all details; although the ancient partnership was changed to a corporation in 1899, the president's load continued as heavy as ever. He felt his responsibilities deeply—once when a bank recommended by the company failed he reimbursed all employees who lost their money. Overwork led to pneumonia and in 1902, Eugene du Pont, last of the black powdermen to head the firm, was dead.

Kaiser Wilhelm and his staff were jubilant as the German Army maneuvered in 1895. They had reason to be: new developments in explosives had strengthened their hand. Alarmed, U. S. Ordnance officials asked Du Pont to make a detailed study of new powders.

SMOKELESS POWDER

During Spanish-American War, troops guarded Carney's Point plant. Here they march through village to set up tents at plant.

IN the early 1880's, hints began to reach the U. S. Army and Navy of a secret armaments race among European chemical laboratories. Observers at army maneuvers of several nations reported that a new principle was being applied to gunpowder. U. S. Ordnance officers called on Du Pont and urged a study.

Presently the secret was out. In 1845 the Swiss chemist Schoenbein had saturated cotton with nitric and sulfuric acids and developed a powerful new explosive. Although he called it "guncotton," it was found to be too violently explosive to handle in guns. Now others had learned to tame this monster and use it as a base for a clean, efficient powder that was flashless and less likely to foul the gun or rifle barrel. They called it smokeless powder.

Soon each European nation was busy developing powder based on the new principle. American powdermakers stood apart from the race; their interest was in civilian, not military, pursuits. The Government, however, finally persuaded Du Pont to undertake manufacture of a military smokeless powder.

At its new explosives plant at Carney's Point, across the Delaware River from Wilmington, the company had already installed, at the Navy's request, facilities to supply guncotton for naval mines and torpedoes. There Francis G. and young Pierre S. du Pont set to work to devise a smoke-

Battleship *Michigan*, left, supervised underwater explosions at Newport, R.I., to test new explosives. Navy early made smokeless powder with Du Pont's help.

Four Leaders in Smokeless Powder

U.S. SIGNAL CORPS

Gen. S. V. Benet,* U. S. Chief of Ordnance, asked Du Pont to investigate smokeless powder.

Christian Schoenbein wiped up nitric acid with wife's apron and so discovered guncotton.

Francis G. du Pont designed machinery for powder, held joint patent covering process.

Pierre S. du Pont as a young man developed process used in making smokeless powder.

less powder. Their first success, in 1893, had proved useful for sportsmen's shotguns, but later a military smokeless powder satisfactory to the Government was found and Du Pont became the country's sole civilian producer. In 1907, when the company was first attacked under the antitrust laws (see page 68), an attempt was made to construe this as a "selfish monopoly." But the Army and Navy soon squelched that, insisting that Du Pont's work on (and responsibility for) smokeless powder was a key to national safety not to be meddled with lightly.

A few years after that, with the world ablaze with war, Du Pont justified its stewardship by supplying over 40 per cent of the military smokeless powder employed by the Allies. More hundreds of millions of pounds were produced for the same purpose in the second World War. Twice, with a product it had undertaken to make as a duty, the company had helped the nation to serve as an arsenal of democracy.

But that was to be only part of the story. Plentiful and cheap cellulose, the starting material of smokeless powder, would in time be directed by Du Pont scientists into hundreds upon hundreds of things for everyday human use: plastics, lacquers, films, fabrics, coatings, and more. Presently these products, issuing from Du Pont plants by trainloads, would be enriching the lives of millions in the U. S.

*General Benet was the father of Stephen Vincent Benét, distinguished American poet.

51

CLOSE OF A CENTURY – AND AN ERA

FOR much of its first century, Du Pont was a partnership. Like most businesses of the time, however, it was run by an individual and for a hundred years it reflected faithfully the person and personality of the senior principal. It was the day of individuality in business as elsewhere. The Carnegie Steel Company was created and managed personally by Andrew Carnegie, the Frick Coal and Coke Company by Henry Frick. That the Du Pont Company was operated by a succession of Messrs. du Pont occasioned little wonder.

But the times were changing. The scale and the complexity of business, particularly in the technical field, pushed well beyond the capacity of a single individual. Amid new conditions, the partnership had weaknesses, not the least of which was the difficulty of preserving the continuity of capable management. Business was turning more and more to the form of a corporation, in which duties, risks and rewards could be more widely shared.

As Du Pont neared the end of its first century, the limitations of the lone hand struck home. Irénée du Pont had been fortunate in finding qualities of leadership in his sons. When Henry du Pont died in 1889, his nephew Eugene, son of Irénée's third son, Alexis, was ready to take over. Thus far, all was well.

But when Eugene du Pont, tired and overworked with the voluminous detail of a modern business, died of pneumonia in 1902, the succession was interrupted. The surviving partners, for various reasons, disqualified themselves. A few months before the hundredth anniversary, they voted that the company was to be sold — to the highest bidder.

"Centennial Gates" were erected at entrance to the Hagley Yards, marking the end of the company's first full century. Symbolically, they were also to bring to a close an era.

THE
MODERN
CORPORATION
1902-1914

THOMAS COLEMAN DU PONT
1902 — 1915

Pierre S. du Pont returned to Brandywine as treasurer of the new corporation. Earlier, he left to join T. Coleman du Pont in Ohio.

Alfred I. du Pont became production chief of the company. He blocked sale of the firm to competitors while he sought cousins' aid.

UNDER NEW MANAGEMENT

AT a side table in the Cafe Savarin, in the old Equitable Building, New York City, coffee cooled in three cups. The trio of young men were too preoccupied with their conversation to notice. First cousins, each was a great-grandson of E. I. du Pont de Nemours. The prospect before them was, therefore, an exciting one. They were planning the purchase — buildings, assets and good name — of the century-old family business. It was quite an undertaking for Thomas Coleman du Pont, 38 (see opposite page), Alfred Irénée du Pont, 37, and Pierre Samuel du Pont, 32.

When the death of Eugene du Pont brought the decision to sell the company, it was expected that the buyer would be Laflin & Rand, Du Pont's strongest rival. All concerned agreed that this was a dismal way to round out a full century of useful achievement, but there appeared to be no help for it.

But help for it there was. Alfred du Pont, a younger member of the firm, sent urgent messages to his cousins, who were occupied elsewhere. The three offered to buy and operate the company, giving notes and stock in a new corporation to be formed. Their offer was warmly accepted, despite the fact that no cash was involved; the business would continue.

At once things began happening. The company's size and variety of

First downtown offices were in Wilmington's only skyscraper on tree-lined street.

activities demanded a division of executive responsibilities and duties. As president, Coleman du Pont assumed charge of expanding and administering the organization. His experience in reorganizing street railways all over the country especially equipped him for this. Alfred du Pont, veteran of years in the yards, became vice president and production chief; Pierre du Pont, treasurer.

From the start the three cousins searched the organization for able associates.* By 1903 they had set up an Executive Committee, to shape overall policy. An incentive system, designed to reward achievement and particularly to encourage ownership of company stock among principal executives, was adopted. A pension plan for all employees codified the informal retirement arrangements that had prevailed since the beginning. Personal responsibility of executives at all grades was established. Obligation, too, was still highly personal: an explosion at a new Indiana plant sent one of the owners speeding west within hours.

The corporation was starting off with a modern outlook, but the lessons of a century on the Brandywine were not to be forgotten. The objective was to blend the yeast of the new with the leavening of the old. It was a recipe well adapted to the healthy appetite of the brand-new Twentieth Century.

*Among those they found: Hamilton Barksdale, H. G. Haskell, Amory Haskell, Charles L. Patterson, Maj. William G. Ramsay.

Teddy Roosevelt went to Panama in 1906 to see how the canal was getting along and posed in a steamshovel. He had reason to be proud: the U. S. was building the canal after France failed. Difference lay in health methods, new explosives and new tools.

AMERICA
COMES OF AGE

IN 1906, President Teddy (*Dee*-lighted!) Roosevelt won the Nobel Peace Prize. This was for calling to a halt the war between Japan and Russia.

The prize did more than bring to the world's official notice a lively American who was already a past master at bringing himself to notice. It also spotlighted the fact (though some nations were later to ignore the warning) that what the world most wanted was peace — peace in which industry and technology could pursue their shared goal of making life more livable for more millions of people. The prize made another point, too: America had now arrived

Chautauqua lectures across the nation brought together large numbers of people to hear serious talk about the U. S. as world power.

Woolworth five-and-ten-cent stores started in these quarters, soon spread over the country, marking beginning of mass distribution.

LIBRARY OF CONGRESS

The American people were beginning to move wider afield; here a Florida beach is shown in early days as an elegant winter resort.

These early planes and the pioneers who flew them presaged era when U. S. would be but a few hours from Europe's capitals.

at full stature in the family of nations, and for better or worse would be required to bear a hand in the family's inevitable squabblings — whether these were over oil rights in some ancient desert or full-dress wars involving hundreds of millions of people. In sum, America was now in full possession of an adult's size, strength — and responsibilities.

Fortunately, development and progress had from the beginning been the nation's chief drives, nor did that change now. Typical of the country's productive attitude to its new international role was the way it took hold of the Panama Canal situation. For years it had been clear

to the world that there should be a canal through the Isthmus of Panama, but no one had got around to building it. America took the job in hand and built the canal. This was more than a benefit to world trade and therefore to the world. It was a demonstration, to Americans and everyone else, that no job that will help make life better for all is too complicated, massive or difficult for a combination of industry, science and old-fashioned courage. In the decades to come, the record both of the country and of the Du Pont Company in doing the seemingly impossible was to prove that point over and over, to the profit of all concerned.

Ford's moving assembly line was prototype of the manufacturing methods that soon would spread into every industry. By 1952, half of U.S. people would earn their livings in businesses not yet known in 1902. Equipment cost was heavy, called for large companies.

MASS PRODUCTION

WHEN the great American consumer wants something, he wants it quickly, in huge quantities and at low cost. It has been so since the country existed.

First it was nails, to help meet the housing shortage that followed, as it has all wars, the Revolution. Returning veterans found hand-wrought nails bringing very fancy prices. In 1795, a man named Perkins solved the problem with a machine that made 60,000 a week.

Next it was muskets, to fight the War of 1812. There were not nearly enough gunsmiths to fill the sudden demand. Eli Whitney devised machines to make the parts separately, in lots of 10,000, then he brought them together to form the whole gun—lock, stock and barrel.

Next it was pins, which then cost as much as 25 cents each and were so rare that housewives used them as a form of barter, or "pin money." Invention of pin-making machinery ended this quaint custom.

Then it was clocks, at the time available only to the wealthy. A production genius named Eli Terry

Early Du Pont mass production move in 1840's was new mill for standardized powder kegs.

built 500 at the same time, of standard design, to sell at a low price. With his partner, a man named Seth Thomas, he created a new industry, based on low costs and mass distribution. Soon every home would have its clock.

Pots and pans yielded next, sold by enterprisers to become famous as Yankee Peddlers. With well-stocked wagons, they drove from settlement to settlement, while craftsmen found means to fill the demands at lower prices.

Later it was hats, clothing, soap, farm equipment and furniture. And by the early 1900's it was something else—the horseless carriage. This was the toughest yet, for even a 1906 car was assembled from hundreds of parts, which had to fit together perfectly.

But another production wizard rose to the occasion. Henry Ford's moving assembly line matched in importance Whitney's theory of interchangeable parts. It made its inventor one of the world's richest men. But the poorest of his customers were to have, as a result, many things denied even the richest of citizens before mass production.

Electric iron—safer, handier than stove-heated irons—speeded and eased housewives' work.

Mass distribution of men's clothing took fine suits out of high-price, hand-tailored class, brought them within range of the average man.

TOWARD BETTER LIVING

TO the housewife of 1910, the pages of *The Saturday Evening Post* opened a new world. Displayed in profusion were exciting advertisements for a variety of new, useful, time-saving articles. Most, a short time before, were luxury items available only to the few. Now large capital investments in mass-production machinery were beginning to bring them within the budget of the many. Some of the wonderful new things the 1910 *Post* reader saw are pictured here. There were scores; soon there would be thousands.

New electric vacuum cleaner was large, noisy, expensive; but it cleaned thoroughly, and required less work than broom or sweeper.

The electric range made its debut and, with the gas stove, virtually abolished the unpredictable, smoke-belching wood-and-coal burner.

Improved canning techniques sent a variety of goods to grocers' shelves. Canned fruit juices were soon to become a national fad.

These Were Chemists

Here, in 1896, is the chemistry faculty and every graduating chemistry student (in aprons) of Yale's Sheffield Scientific School.* Chemists were then as eagerly sought as hard-hitting outfielders.

In 1912, entire personnel of Du Pont Experimental Station, numbering less than 70, assembled for this photograph. Most of their experiments were directed towards finding new uses for cellulose.

Pioneers at Eastern Laboratory, company's first formal research unit, included: back, from left: C. F. Lindsay, R. T. Cann, J. W. McCoy, W. O. Heard; front: C. L. Reese, S. Emery, J. B. Bronstein.

By 1912 a collection of buildings took form at the Experimental Station, many of them refurbished powder mills bunched along the Brandywine.

PLANNED RESEARCH

DURING Du Pont's first hundred years, the application of science to mankind's needs had been the responsibility of a succession of lone experts. But now both the science and the needs had become so complex that no one person could hope to bring them together. From now on research men would work most effectively in teams, with organized plans before them and money behind them.

The new corporation was one of the first American companies to perceive and face up to this fact. In 1902, it set up at Repauno its first formal research venture, Eastern Laboratory, and assigned it the task of improving explosives and techniques for making them. The next year an even more significant venture was launched. A second research laboratory, christened the Experimental Station, was established in its own building on the Brandywine. Its assignment soon indicated the trend of the new management's thinking; going beyond the traditional emphasis on explosives, the Station's small band of chemists and engi-

*In 1951, U. S. college science faculties numbered 44,000; science and engineering students graduated: 85,000.

The quiet atmosphere was occasionally shattered by shots from adjoining trap-shooting club. Spire of Christ Church still looked down at scene.

Francis I. du Pont was first director of Experimental Station. He was trained at Yale, had part in smokeless powder development.

Potbellied stove for winter warmth was feature of early Du Pont plant control laboratory, occupied by Chemist Sidney Emery. It contrasts sharply with today's ultra-modern laboratory facilities.

Laboratory equipment at the company's first Experimental Station, started in 1903, featured bare slabs, gas lighting, the simplest kind of apparatus. Despite this, it was the most up-to-date of its day.

First Experimental Station laboratory was this building, later burned, on the Brandywine. It started in life as the Rokeby cotton mill, then served as a practice hall for a fife and drum corps.

neers was to range over the entire chemical field, looking for new opportunities. Ample financial support was placed at their disposal; by 1906, $300,000 a year, a huge sum in those days, was going into Du Pont research. On the site of the old Brandywine yards (old powder mills are still standing along the creek), a group of laboratories grew up and slowly a staff was assembled.

Long-range planning was required—later on a program of fellowships was started to encourage graduate study in the sciences at universities. But, starting with a small group, research began on lacquers, artificial leather, plastics and photographic film; as early as 1909 Du Pont chemists were pushing into the field which Du Pont has since made so familiar in everyday American life—synthetic fibers. Outside laboratory windows, the Brandywine coursed idly over Henry Clay dam, no longer harnessed to the wheels. But as it had to other Du Pont men through the years, the stream murmured its soft encouragement.

Tar-surfaced roads softened in hot weather, spattered car finishes. Du Pont's new laboratories produced a remedy advertised here.

Ads of the day showed trend of Du Pont's diversification after 1910. First important new product to be sold was coated fabrics.

Lacquers, a field which Du Pont first entered in 1904, were to provide a base that would lead to a whole new range of finishes.

LIBRARY OF CONGRESS

With more leisure, people took advantage of resorts, where they got ankles wet and showed off new dresses. Horizons of Americans were broadening; demands were increasing; a new way of life was opening. Du Pont saw these changes as offering new opportunities.

INTO
NEW FIELDS

Expanding auto industry provided ready market for new products. Coated fabric car tops were advertised as "very strong."

BY the early 1900's, Du Pont had long been familiar with the raw materials of explosives—nitric acid, cellulose and guncotton. A great future lay ahead in developing these materials into new and useful products, but obvious handicaps stood in the way. In both production and sales, Du Pont experience was limited to explosives.

The management plan was to direct its new research program along lines of consumer interest. If this was to be meaningful, it would require a commercial experience against which results might be gauged. The quickest way to acquire the necessary background was to buy it on the open market—in established firms that had been offered for sale.

This process had begun, in 1904, as a by-product of the purchase of the International Smokeless Powder and Chemical Co. In its plant at Parlin, N. J., this firm produced numerous nitrocellulose solutions and an excellent lacquer widely used on brass hardware and the brass beds of the day.

Now came, in 1910, acquisition of the first non-explosives firm, the Fabrikoid Co., producers of a kind of artificial leather, made by treating cotton cloth with coatings of a nitrocellulose solution. This was followed by purchase of the Arlington Co., makers of nitrocellulose or "pyroxylin" plastics. Next the Fairfield Rubber Co. was brought in, amplifying the existing line of coated fabrics. A number of minor firms in the finishes trade joined the list, which shortly was to include the noted Harrison's Inc., an old producer of paints and chemicals.

Presently an improved (and less odoriferous) artificial leather was appearing on thousands of automobiles, which at the time used a fabric panel on the roof of closed models, and was doing well in luggage, handbags and bookbindings. Ladies were charmed by the appearance of plastic "dresser sets," including buttonhook and pin tray, which were sold under exotic titles like "Du Barry" and "Sheraton." Du Pont lacquers, enamels and finishes began to come to market.

The framework for development was being assembled deliberately, piece by piece, each section in its assigned relationship to the others and to the whole. Eventually, with the skeleton complete, research was to flesh out the bones.

Improved coated fabric for auto tops occupied chemists. Rayntite marked advance.

Celluloid collars and cuffs* were boon to men, could be cleaned without ill effect.

Paints were added to Du Pont's line of lacquers, broadening the company's base.

Few cars were closed. Vexing problem of brittle curtains was helped by new cement.

Du Pont cement became household word, for it solved innumerable home problems.

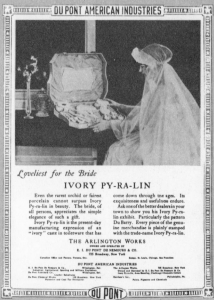

Chemists' continuing efforts to match and excel nature were reflected in new plastics.

*Celluloid dickies, or false shirt fronts, were another Du Pont product. The Leominster, Mass., plant produced celluloid bibs for nuns until well into the 1930's.

BRANDYWINE POWDERMEN

THESE wise and earnest faces reflect an industrial era that belongs to the past. Each was a Brandywine powderman, whose skill, care and devotion helped build a nation. Bearers of a proud tradition, many are sons of pow-

Charles Beatty, whose father worked on the Brandywine before him, was born in 1875, started in the mills as a carpenter at 16. Later he helped build first laboratories at Experimental Station.

John Bue, born in Italy in 1881, came to the U. S. in 1907. At the Du Pont mills many other new Americans—Italian and Irish—were also employed. Powderman then worked a 10-hour day.

Elias Rutter, born in 1882, went into mills as World War I started. Demands were so great that he often worked 14 hours a day. He recalls company's first automobile, a Chevrolet bought in 1915.

Harry E. Lee, born in 1882, began as a powderman in 1906, later went to Experimental Station. One of his jobs: carrying in nitroglycerin from a cache in woods, where it was stored for safety.

dermen and grew up within sound of the running stream that turned the mills well into the Twentieth Century.*

Although the yards where the men worked have long been silent with disuse, each of these veteran craftsmen was in vigorous health in 1952, when these photographs were taken. Nothing could illustrate so aptly the speed of modern development, which in a single generation has proceeded from water wheels to hopeful talk of atomic power.

Edward Bader, born in 1873, came to the mills as machinist in 1896. He built the "Centennial" gates and, in 1904, constructed the company's first gas-driven locomotive, which replaced horses.

Joseph Haley, born in 1875, came to work in 1898. He became a "Black Boss"—a powder foreman making daily inspection trips through mills. A son and two sons-in-law now work for Du Pont.

James Poinsett, born in 1874, started work in 1913, when more than 95 per cent of Du Pont explosives went for non-military uses. A year later he was working 14 hours a day on Allied war orders.

PHOTOS BY HANS KNOPF

Charles Godfrey went to work at the mills on the Brandywine in 1907, when he was 16. There he packed and weighed kegs, wore powderman's shoes fastened with wooden pegs instead of nails.

*Water power had its shortcomings. One old powderman recalls that the four seasons to a water man were made up of freshets in the spring, drought in the summer, leaves in the fall, and ice all winter long.

John J. Walsh was 18 years old and looked like this when he went to work for the Fabrikoid Co. at Newburgh, N. Y., in 1908, two years before Du Pont acquired it. Then, plant had about 75 people.

INDUSTRY ACQUIRES A NEW KIND OF EMPLOYEE

Today, John Walsh is a sales service supervisor at Newburgh. Plant now employs 10 times as many people as in 1910.

THE powderman of the Brandywine in many ways typified the individual Nineteenth Century artisan; part craftsman, part technician, part skilled professional. Such workmen were proud and substantial citizens, but their productivity was limited. The machinery at their command was still crude; much of their work was done by hand. And what held for powder held also for shoes, clothing, furniture and other consumer needs.

Now for the first time there came into the company an employee not trained on explosives. This was the early prototype of the industrial worker, whose contribution lay not so much in long experience as with his understanding of the output - multiplying machinery just beginning to make its appearance. It came to Du Pont notably with the purchase of the Fabrikoid Company, of Newburgh, N. Y., in 1910.

Typical of this new type was John J. Walsh, then a young operator. The new industrial revolution was yet to spread its blessings: Walsh's earnings approximated $9 for a 50-hour week.* With resources to develop ingenious new machines and assembly lines, large business units were now to turn out consumer products at a fraction of their old cost. Up to this time, most of the production benefits had gone to the consumer in lower prices. But soon the centrifugal force of the cycle was to hurl the gains in all directions. And the industrial worker, in reduced hours, job stability and increased wages, was in time to reap the harvest.

"Village Industry," painting by Stanhope Forbes, shows how most consumer goods still were made by individual craftsmen.

*Shorter than average; hours in 1910 still ran up to 60 per week. By 1952, American workers would have, in reduced working time, the equivalent of 150 paid holidays yearly when compared to 19th Century standards.

These fabric coating machines and the men and women who operated them at the Fabrikoid Co. brought new and different skills to the Du Pont Company. They produced 5 yards a man-hour. Later improved machines would boost that figure to almost 15 yards and bring lower prices, higher wages. This was new pattern of industry.

Women workers came into Du Pont employ in numbers for first time with the opening of the Pompton Lakes, N. J., plant.* Aside from the textile and needle trades, factories had few female jobs.

In 1910, automobiles were a novelty. Most employees rode bikes or trolleys or walked to work. When Fabrikoid president acquired new Buick, employees exhibited normal curiosity. Walsh is at crank.

*Women of the du Pont family, however, were partners in the business from the early days on the Brandywine until 1902, and had thus participated in the company's management.

DIVISION
BY
DECREE

Farewell banquet for those employees who were leaving Du Pont to organize Hercules and Atlas Powder Companies was given at New Willard Hotel, Washington, D.C., in 1912.

COMPETITION between business firms in the Nineteenth Century developed largely around the basic, indispensable commodities: iron, coal, lumber and, to an extent, powder. Still to come was the time when most of these would be challenged in at least part of their market by competitive materials—coal by oil, steel by aluminum, lumber by cheaper metals and masonry, powder by better explosives and earth-moving machinery. For the time being, the course of expansion was full-speed ahead.

In the swarming, frontier-breaking years that followed the Civil War, the greatest problem, and greatest need, was production. In many fields, one answer seemed to lie in combination. One large producing unit, it was argued, could operate more efficiently than a dozen small in the same line, and through its size effect economies in manufacture otherwise impossible. The result was a period of consolidations and mergers unprecedented in history.

In the late Eighties, the nation took alarm at the scale and the direction of this movement. The dissent was marked, in 1890, by passage of the Sherman Anti-Trust Act.* .

Du Pont through this period stood apart from the tide. "We manage our own business in every particular and allow no trusts or combinations to rule or dictate what we shall do," the head of the firm stated in the Eighties. The company had, however, helped to organize, in 1827, a group known as the Gunpowder Trade Association. This was not a "trust" in the legal sense as its members operated independently, though it later acquired that description. It was formed originally to remedy practices which were disrupting the powder industry. Many local mills had sprung up during the Civil War while the larger companies were occupied with military production. When peace came, these mills fought desperately for survival. Wild price cutting, secret rebates and bribery threw the business into turmoil. Du Pont and two other established firms joined together as competitors to stand against the offenders.

Gradually Du Pont began to broaden its scope by buying into other powder companies which served some particular locality. When the new management took charge of the company in 1902, they found that they owned wholly or partially a number of properties far removed from the Brandywine. The arrangements were confused and complicated. The new corporation simplified the situation by bringing the outlying affiliations into the Du Pont Company, buying out minority interests in some cases and in others acquiring full ownership of additional producing units. Two years after they took over the leadership, they dissolved the old Gunpowder Trade Association.

The Sherman Act at this time had been in effect little more than a decade. It was still a controversial issue, even among the judiciary: Mr. Justice Holmes, although the most "liberal" member of the Supreme Court, had described it as an "unworkable monstrosity." The body of law that was growing out of court decisions was slow in taking shape; there were grave questions, as yet undetermined, as to its applicability in any given case.

In 1907 the Government filed suit against Du Pont, charging violation of the anti-trust laws in explosives.

The resultant court action strung on for four years. The ashes of the defunct Trade Association were raked and sifted and forgotten tales retold as hundreds of witnesses filled thirteen volumes of testimony. In 1911, the court held that Du Pont's share of the explosives business was "dominance of the industry" and in restraint of trade.

The company's explosives business was accordingly cut up into three parts. Du Pont retained twelve black powder mills, five dynamite plants, and three smokeless powder plants. The rest was divided between two new independent corporations, the Hercules Powder Company and the Atlas Powder Company.

Witnesses representing the U. S. Army and Navy provided a curiously realistic aftermath to the proceedings. They insisted to the court that Du Pont's smokeless powder facilities be maintained intact. To this official appeal the court agreed, decreeing, "No benefit would accrue to the public by dividing this business between several competing concerns, while injury to public interests of a grave character might and probably would result therefrom."

*The "trust" was a legal instrument enabling a group of companies to join together by assigning their assets to a trusteeship which would act for all. Public disapproval of the device was so marked that the dictionary took note and hastily amended its definition from "confidence, belief, truth, hope; expectation" (Webster's, 1853) to "a combination formed for the purpose of controlling a trade or business by doing acts in restraint of trade." (Webster's, 1882.) Original "trust" was outlawed early.

WORLD WAR I
1914-1918

First German troops goose-stepped into Brussels and spiked helmet became grim symbol of Teutonic terror. It was to be three years before America entered war.

WAR IN EUROPE

Most of U. S. press quickly chose Allied side. Cartoonists tried to outdo each other in detailing the Hun's barbarities. Kaiser replaced Mexico's Pancho Villa as most hated man.

IN the hot summer of 1914, a fanatical Serbian nationalist shot an Austrian Archduke and within a few days millions of Europeans were in arms and on the march.

President Wilson quickly proclaimed American neutrality, but most Americans had already committed their sympathies. Germany's brutal and unprovoked attack on "brave little Belgium" had touched off the tinder box, and the American press indulged its full capacity for indignation against German *Kultur*.

Du Pont officials doubted that the war would last, though they were disturbed over impending shortages of imported materials (see cuts). Smokeless powder, which for the first time was to figure in actual warfare, would be consumed quickly by machine guns and the quick-firing French 75's, which were also making their debut in action. It looked as though the Allies would run out long before the Germans. Smokeless powder production in those times was slow and large-scale facilities for its manufacture existed neither here nor in England. Beyond that, nitrates for Allied powder had to come thousands of miles from Chile, through submarine-infested waters.* The Germans had forehandedly solved this problem. Dr. Fritz Haber had developed a process for extracting nitrogen from the air; by 1915 it was operating. With exports from America forbidden, few experts this side of the ocean believed the Allies would be able to keep guns firing long enough to survive.

Du Pont smokeless powder facilities were soon swamped by frantic Allied pleas for more powder to meet well-equipped Germans. Quick Du Pont expansion helped stem the tide.

Three Headlines with a Meaning for the Future

POWDER IS LACKING FOR LONG CONFLICT

duPont Officials Say European Supply Would'nt Last Armies Six Months

LONG WAR NOT LOOKED FOR BY POWDERMAKERS

A general war in Europe could not

A "short war," due to small supplies of smokeless powder, was forecast by Du Pont.

DUPONTS SEEK HOME SUPPLY OF POTASH

War Shuts Off German Shipments, Now Look to Washington State

WILL UTILIZE HELP ALONG PUGET SOUND

As a result of the European war,

U. S. dependence on German chemicals was emphasized when war cut off imports.

THE WAR BOOSTS DRUG PRICES

Some Foreign Products Have Been Withdrawn From the Market.

THE SUPPLY IS SHORT

American Laboratories May be Able to Produce Good Substitutes.

The possibility of a famine in this

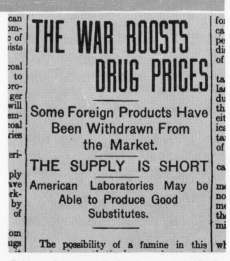

Prices of imported drugs went sky-high. Many drugs, including aspirin, disappeared.

*Only the epic Battle of the Falkland Islands, off the coast of South America, in which much of the German surface navy was destroyed by the British, enabled it to come at all.

European purchasing missions, like this French group shown with Marshal Joffre, became familiar sights in U. S. as Allies sought aid. First Du Pont powder contract was signed with the Russians.

DU PONT GOES TO THE ALLIES' AID

New efficiency measures, like this overhead trolley to carry supplies, were added to Du Pont facilities.This device was installed at Haskell plant.

EMBARGO of aid to the Allied cause was short-lived under the pressure of public opinion. Soon the peaceful small-town atmosphere of Wilmington was enlivened by the arrival of foreign diplomats accompanied by officers in picturesque uniforms. These were the purchasing missions from France, England and Russia, come to seek Du Pont aid.

Contrary to the theme which would be raised later, their proposals aroused little enthusiasm. Du Pont was busy with peacetime affairs; to supply powder would mean deferring its development indefinitely. Furthermore, no one yet believed the war could last long, and new powder lines would stand useless when peace returned.*

The Allied cause, however, was desperate, and finally an agreement was reached. Du Pont agreed to supply the powder, the Allies covering the cost of new facilities in the price of the powder. This was set initially at a dollar a pound, which would come down as building costs were amortized.

The expansion that now got underway was the most rapid the company had known. Production of TNT and caps and fuses was multiplied; plants at Carney's Point, Haskell and Parlin in New Jersey were enlarged until they employed 16,000 men and women. Even this was not enough; still more facilities and employees would be needed to meet increasing demands.

War demands required training new employees like these at the Haskell plant. Employment in the company's own plants rose from 5500 in 1914 to more than 55,000 in 1918.

Caps and fuses were made at Pompton Lakes, which normally produced blasting supplies. Employment jumped from 300 to 7500; peak daily output reached 1,500,000 caps.

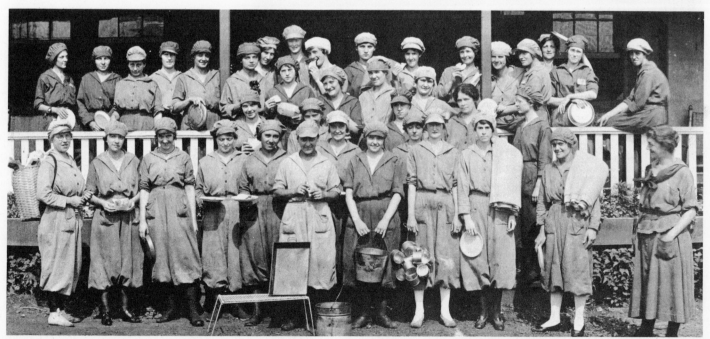

Carney's Point powder girls helped boost plant's smokeless powder production from 12,000 to 900,000 pounds a day. By time U.S. entered war, Du Pont had produced 400 million pounds of smokeless powder. By Armistice Day, total was 1,398,700,000 pounds.

*Only possible use for an explosives plant: making explosives.

THIS GUNCOTTON PLANT DU PONT BUILT AND OPERATED AT HOPEWELL, VA., WAS LARGEST OF ITS KIND IN

MIRACLE AT HOPEWELL

Hopewell Village was built from the ground up to house the employees at the plant, most of whom came from other parts of U. S. and needed shelter. Company built facilities for 1850 families, dormitories for single men, schools, churches, streets, shopping facilities.

WORLD, TURNED OUT MORE THAN 1 BILLION POUNDS OF MATERIAL, EMPLOYED MORE THAN 28,000 PEOPLE.

KEY ingredient of smokeless powder is nitrocellulose. At the outbreak of war in 1914, Du Pont had facilities for making less than a million pounds of it a month. Long before the war ended, output was over a million and a half pounds a *day*.

Scene of this production miracle was Hopewell, Virginia, where Du Pont had recently built a new dynamite plant. Thousands of workers converged on the site, where they had to be sheltered and fed. A disastrous fire wiped out sections of the town. But with unbelievable speed, facilities were built for making sulfuric and nitric acids, for purifying cotton linters, and for converting them into nitrocellulose.

Hopewell plant staff,* recruited from other Du Pont operations, accomplished unprecedented job in creating new facilities for guncotton and in training 28,000 men and women, virtually all of whom were newcomers to the explosives industry, for their exacting jobs.

*Front row, left to right: R. E. Kendall, W. M. Johnson, E. N. Johnson, R. G. Clough, W. P. Allen, plant manager; C. K. Davis, F. C. Evans, D. W. Brown, E. S. Higgins. Back row, left to right: J. T. Smith, F. C. Kennedy, F. Tyson, G. LeFebvre, H. E. Mecredy, L. S. Bitner, S. Groves, H. F. Eigenbrodt, P. N. Webb, T. B. Baker.

Employees of "Fabrikoid" plant in Newburgh paraded down city's main street in 1918 to give drafted co-workers a hearty send-off. More than 8500 Du Pont employees joined armed forces during World War I; number was to top 38,000 in World War II.

Plant security was vital. At Old Hickory, above, Tennessee Militia and company guard force shared the task of protecting the employees and the prop-

U. S. ENTERS THE WAR

THE switch from "Preparedness" to participation in the war called on Du Pont for still greater production efforts. What had already been accomplished was, for the day, an incredible performance. As war broke in 1914, military explosives had represented barely five per cent of Du Pont gross earnings; yet, as early as 1916, General Hedlam, chief of the British Munitions Board, was reporting, "The Du Pont Company is entitled to the credit of saving the British Army." This was, of course, in addition to the help given France, Russia and Italy, which had come into the war on the Allied side. Now the United States also needed Du Pont's help, and the company was asked to take on five additional major projects. The first four were a shell-loading plant at Penniman, Va.; a high explosives plant at Racine, Wis.; and the operation of new plants for

On This Day 12,500 War Workers Lined Up at

erty. So far as is known, no significant act of sabotage was committed on any Du Pont-operated plant during either World War. Careful screening processes helped.

Liberty Bond rallies were held at Du Pont locations. Arlington employees, above, turned out to hear military officials. Through the company alone, Du Pont employees purchased more than $1 million worth of Liberty Bonds and War Savings Stamps.

bag-loading powder at Tullytown, Pa., and Seven Pines, Va.

But the fifth of the additional assignments was something much more difficult: to build and operate the largest smokeless powder plant the world had ever seen—and a complete town to go with it. This was the largest military project undertaken up to that time (see below).

Plant and town shared the name "Old Hickory," and were built near Nashville, Tenn. Seven miles of railroad had to be laid to take building materials to the site. Production of sulfuric acid began 67 days after ground-breaking, nitric acid 9 days later, guncotton, the raw material of smokeless powder, two weeks after that. The first finished powder was granulated 116 days after the breaking of ground for the plant, 121 days ahead of contract agreement.

It took a total of 30,000 men and women to operate the

plant, recruited everywhere. Most were new to powder-making and had to be trained by Du Pont personnel.

Almost all had also to be housed. The complete town Du Pont built included 3867 buildings—dwellings, apartment houses, hotels, restaurants, schools, churches, theaters, hospitals, a city hall, fire and police stations. Miles of paved streets, sidewalks, water lines and sewers were laid. All this was in addition to the 1112 buildings comprising the powder plant, a 540-foot steel suspension bridge over the Cumberland River, and double-tracking of the 7-mile railroad to handle 1100 cars and 31,000 passengers daily.

For operating the plant Du Pont received a fee based on output—after taxes it came to 1 per cent of value of product made. But for building this huge project, Du Pont sent the Government an odd bill. The price: a single dollar.

Paymasters' Booths to Get Their Weekly Wage

Sidelights of the War:

Women's Munition Reserve recruited war workers. These were in Brandywine yards.

German propaganda, designed to lure war workers from jobs, was scotched by cartoons.

"All the News That's Fit to Print." The New

VOL. LXVIII...NO. 22,206. .... NEW YORK, MOND

ARMISTICE SIGNI
BERLIN SEIZED
NEW CHANCELLO
OUSTED KAISEI

VICTORY

PUSH THE JOB

HELP FILL THE EMPTY SHELL

GIVE THE KAISER —

Plant posters urged Old Hickory, Tenn., workers on by inviting revenge on Kaiser.

AMERICA'S GREATEST INDUSTRIAL OPPORTUNITY

HOPEWELL VIRGINIA

DU PONT CHEMICAL COMPANY
INCORPORATED
WILMINGTON, DELAWARE

DU PONT

At war's end, Du Pont left Hopewell but helped develop area for peacetime industry.

THE war ended as suddenly as it had begun. On November 11, 1918, Du Pont stood with $260 million in unfinished Government contracts. Eager to get back to civilian production, the company asked and received quick cancellation of all military commitments, at no profit to itself.

The war record had been a proud one. Du Pont had supplied over 40 per cent — 1,466,761,219 pounds — of the standard explosives used on the Allied side, plus millions of pounds of specialized explosives, caps and fuses.

As Du Pont people rejoiced at the return of peace and of loved ones in

Reddest-faced man, Chancellor Bethmann-Hollweg, guessed U. S. too weak to fight.

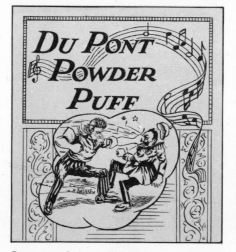

DU PONT POWDER PUFF

Song popular at Old Hickory failed to sweep nation but upped the plant's morale.*

This was Du Pont's Executive Committee, at the close of the war, in picture taken shortly before

*Typical lyrics, sung to the tune of *Coming Through the Rye*, were: "Old Hickory plant is working nights to make the real stuff, To paste upon the Kaiser's nose —a Du Pont Powder Puff."

k Times.

THE WEATHER
Fair today and Tuesday: diminish-
ing northwest winds.

TWENTY-FOUR PAGES.   TWO CENTS Metropolitan District   THREE CENTS   FOUR CENTS
                                  50 Mile Radius   Within 200 Miles   Elsewhere

ND OF THE WAR!
EVOLUTIONISTS;
EGS FOR ORDER;
ES TO HOLLAND

AND PEACE

military service, the company itself issued its own word of gratification. Peace, not war, was the Du Pont horizon, now as it had always been.

Pierre S. du Pont pointed out that up to the start of the war Du Pont had been in business 113 years, of which only 8½ could be called war years; that even during the war, annual commercial sales had risen from $26 million to $72 million. The company's size and strength — in organization, manpower and resources — had enabled it to adjust quickly to wartime needs. Now those same factors facilitated return to a peacetime economy.

At all Du Pont plants, war's end was greeted with relief and celebrations. Pompton Lakes, N. J., workers formed a motorcade, painted crude signs, snaked through the town.

its last meeting in April, 1919.* Younger men who had proved themselves in the gruelling war years took over. Irénée du Pont replaced his brother, Pierre S. du Pont, as president. Pierre became Du Pont board chairman and president of General Motors.

*Standing, left to right: F. W. Pickard, Lammot du Pont, R. R. M. Carpenter, H. Fletcher Brown, F. Donaldson Brown, Committee Secretary M. D. Fisher; seated: Frank L. Connable, William Coyne, Pierre S. du Pont, Irénée du Pont, H. G. Haskell, F. G. Tallman. Of these, all except F. W. Pickard, Lammot du Pont and F. Donaldson Brown retired from the Executive Committee in April, 1919.

The Auto in Its Infancy

Model T cost $850 in 1908, was very popular, had but one function: to transport people economically from one place to another.

Most autos in early days were luxury models. This 1907 Matheson sold for $5500.* Its comforts were unavailable in low-priced cars.

Motoring was adventure in 1914. Few roads were hard surfaced; autos often became mired. Tires and batteries were unreliable.

The Early Steps Toward a Mature

A mass-produced Chevrolet that combined economy with style and comfort is shown by G.M. officials. (William Knudsen at right.)

THE G. M. VENTURE

Du Pont brought to General Motors financial stability and managerial leadership.† Now, four Du Pont officers sit on G.M. Board.

*For an additional $250 you could get a top.

†Pierre S. du Pont, fourth from left above, was G.M. president, 1920-1923. Flanking him in picture are John J. Raskob, right, who resigned from Du Pont Executive Committee to become chairman of G.M. Finance Committee; and Alfred P. Sloan, G.M. vice president, who succeeded Mr. du Pont as G.M. president and later became board chairman.

Refinement in interior appointments such as fine upholstery and stylish trim now became available for cars in every price class.

Buying cars on time was introduced by General Motors in 1919, greatly extending auto market. Note the premium on closed cars.

IN 1915, the fledgling giant that was the U. S. automobile industry was little more than a decade old, and had been subject to more than its share of childhood illnesses. It was a wobbly if promising infant, shaky on its feet and badly in need of parental sympathy, which meant backers with faith, background and cash. There were dozens of small companies (over 2000 different makes have been offered U. S. motorists since 1900), many headed by brilliant inventors or mechanics with little business experience. Banks and lending agencies preferred sounder risks.

A shrewd organizer named William C. Durant was an exception to the norm. He was one of the first to see the automobile as a national institution. In 1908, he had founded a company called General Motors, but his dreams of a car to every family were too far advanced for his supporters. In 1910, he left active management.

Du Pont officials, to whom Durant later told his story, agreed with his predictions of a great industry. The early years of World War I had made it necessary for Du Pont to build up a large financial and managerial organization; here was a chance to make it of service in a useful peacetime pursuit. As a result of large investments in the then-independent Chevrolet Motor Co., Durant was reinstated at General Motors, and Du Pont became a major stockholder.*

The end of the war was to bring an acute crisis to the industry. Again Du Pont funds were made available, in part to rescue Durant, who had become heavily involved. He then stepped aside as president and from 1920 until 1923, Pierre du Pont personally took charge. A new policy was introduced. The early idea of utility alone in the low-priced car was abandoned; Chevrolet, the G. M. entry, was to introduce style and comfort—eventually it set a trend that all were to follow.

But with this, Du Pont turned management back to the auto men at Detroit and Alfred P. Sloan became president. Henceforth Du Pont was to regard its participation in the automobile field as it had in the beginning: an investment in a promising and productive segment of America's future.

What Became of These?

TOOL BOX in constant use because service stations were few and cars unreliable?

PATCH KIT for emergency repairs before rubber chemicals prolonged life of tires?

ACETYLENE TANK for gas to light the risky lamps of foolhardy night drivers?

*In all, some $50 million was invested in the motor venture. Today, Du Pont owns 20,000,000 shares, or just under 23 per cent, of the outstanding stock of General Motors Corporation. In the post-war crisis Du Pont borrowed money to assist G.M., the only time since the earliest days that it resorted to a loan. It was speedily repaid.

continued on next page

The Auto Today

G.M. contributions, as typified by this 1952 model, provided low-cost, efficient transportation in a variety of sizes, colors, styles.

Auto manufacture gives employment to 900,000 people; auto sales and services employ 2,000,000. Indirect employment: 6,500,000.

Auto industry opened vast new fields of opportunity for the small businessman, especially in gas stations, sales, tires, accessories.

P. S. DU PONT RESIGNS AS GEN. MOTORS HEAD

Leaves Presidency to Become Chairman of Board of Directors.

The resignation of Pierre S. du Pont as president and chairman of the executive committee of the General Motors Corporation was announced yesterday in New York. Alfred P. Sloan, Jr., was elected as his successor.

G.M. had sound organizational and financial basis by 1923; P.S. du Pont retired as president.

AS the mass-produced automobile became available to more and more millions, the industry it created spread its roots far and wide. Within thirty years some 10,000,000 people were to make their livings along the trail blazed by the once-despised horseless carriage. Large assembly plants relied literally upon thousands of suppliers of goods and services. More and better roads meant employment and opportunities for men to engineer and build them. More and better gasolines and oils were needed—and people to produce and sell them. Tires and accessories themselves became big business, with their own circles of suppliers and sub-contractors. Anti-freezes, upholstery yard goods, paints and polishes were added. There were filling stations, garages, roadside restaurants, places to stay overnight—and people to finance, build and man them. Calvin Coolidge had said that the business of America was business. The mass-produced automobile was just beginning to prove how the benefits of one business could be spread about.

To accommodate a nation on wheels,* more than a million miles of new roads have been built since 1925, many of them superhighways.

*Today, 40,000,000 families own a car, and 3,500,000 families more than one. Average U. S. car travels over 10,000 miles a year, more than the typical 1900 family traveled in a decade.

An Album
of
Leadership

Five Who Have Served Du Pont
As Its President in the Modern Era
In Striking Contemporary Portraits

© KARSH

PIERRE SAMUEL DU PONT

Honorary Chairman of the Board
President, 1915-1919

Biographers have described Pierre du Pont as one of the business giants responsible for American industrial pre-eminence and as the ablest member of his clan since the founder. In the inner circles of the company, only he would demur, for no man is so greatly respected, no man has won wider affection. Yet his modest, self-effacing demeanor shuns the spotlight, and he is quick to credit others with the unique contributions he has made. Born in 1870, close to the Brandywine yards, he brought to the company a breadth and vigor which served, long after his retirement from active affairs, as an inspiration and example to all who were to follow.

IRÉNÉE DU PONT

President, 1919-1926

During his long association with the company, Irénée du Pont has both smashed and set precedents. Born in 1876, he took an engineering degree from M.I.T., but chose to begin his career as a mechanic in a machine shop. Soon after becoming president, he recast management procedures into their present committee form, in effect abdicating the centralized power of the presidency. And at 49 he retired, with the explanation, "I'm slowing up," shaping a policy which has revitalized upper management by sifting younger men continually toward the top. Known as "Bus" to family and intimates, he exudes a gregarious, good-humored charm.

© KARSH

85

HANS KNOPF

LAMMOT DU PONT

President, 1926-1940

Lammot du Pont, born in 1880, added to an M.I.T. degree the trade of black powderman, acquired on the Brandywine. Learning to work with his hands gave him a respect and feeling for tools; he likes to chop wood and sharpen the family cutlery on an old treadle stone. Motorists often see him bicycling to work amid heavy traffic. Simple and direct, he has a candor that wins the regard even of those who disagree most with his views. Soon after he came to the presidency in 1926, it became his task to guide the company through the readjustments of the Thirties. When he passed along the helm, the great storm had been well weathered.

WALTER SAMUEL CARPENTER, JR.

Chairman of the Board
President, 1940-1948

Walter S. Carpenter, Jr., was the first president of the company unrelated to the du Pont family. Leaving college early, he had started with the firm as a cub engineer on construction and at 32 was named to the Executive Committee. His career since has revealed every reason for this meteoric rise. His presidency spanned the crucial war years and the early period of post-war expansion, assignments calling for the utmost of tact, delicacy and finely-shaded judgment. Personally, he is noted for his grave, unfailing courtesy, his quiet sense of humor and a lively interest in many topics, including, in baseball season, daily scores by innings.

HANS KNOPF

87

CRAWFORD HALLOCK GREENEWALT

President, 1948-

Crawford H. Greenewalt became president in 1948. After graduation from M.I.T., he started work as a chemist and has never lost his scientific interest. Although notable technical contributions have marked his rise to the top, it is as a poised and articulate champion of enterprise that he has met the challenge of the times. Quick to probe to the nub of perplexing public questions, he is equally skillful at presenting his case. His interests range broadly; he discusses weighty economic problems with the same ease that he chats about favorite avocations like color photography or music; reads with equal zest Gibbon and chilling detective thrillers.

NEW
FRONTIERS
1919-1939

Women exercised new voting privilege not only in political elections but in new employee representation groups, as in first "Works Council" balloting at Arlington plant in 1920. Councils were labor-management groups formed to iron out employee relations problems. In most cases, Councils were replaced later by local independent unions selected by employees.

A WOMAN'S WORLD

Helen Wills, national tennis heroine, led parade of women into sports world, where they soon called for new kinds of clothing.

Radio brought women closer to world events, brought advertisers closer to women, especially when "soap operas" became the rage.

THE decade of the 1920's was featured by the dramatic mass emergence of many interesting phenomena, including the automobile, the radio, the motion picture, and woman. Most, including woman, had been around for some time: only now did the scene suddenly swarm with them.

Most conspicuous of the emergees was, of course, woman. Having won the right to vote, she went on to bright new victories. The 19th Amendment gave her the vote, the rest she did herself. Sparked by blithe spirits like Gertrude Ederle, Helen Wills and Amelia Earhart, her accomplishments made headlines. Except in a few die-hard establishments, she routed the male stenographer from offices and took her place in the business world. Movie fans, brought up on Mary Pickford and Mary Miles Minter, had always known woman was sweet; Gloria Swanson and Phyllis Haver showed she could be glamorous. Women learned to drive cars, to the delight of cartoonists, and feminine smoking no longer was regarded as wicked. Cigarette sales jumped from 47 billion in 1920 to 125 billion in 1930.

Particularly striking was the change in woman's appearance. Skirts rose from the ankle to the knee. Girdles replaced corsets and underwear became filmy lingerie. Hosiery, now conspicuous, was of sheer silk in beige or flesh tints. Lipstick became as common as face powder in the average woman's handbag. She bobbed her hair and painted—and repainted—her finger nails. The American woman burst free of the political, financial and social bonds in which man and ladylike reserve had long confined her.

Up to this time industry had for the most part served woman chiefly by indirection. But now she wanted a larger wardrobe, numerous changes of costume to match her speedy pace. In her home she demanded better equipment and better foods. She wanted improved and more colorful fabrics, finishes and paints. In fact, now that she had the asking power, there was almost no end to the good things woman demanded of industry, and especially its chemical branch. Having served with distinction the nation's pioneers, protectors and builders, Du Pont and chemistry now prepared to face up to this new and exacting challenge of the Twenties.*

*"What really makes Du Pont, the company, live and breathe is—women!" says John Gunther in his "Inside U.S.A.," written in 1947."Its history is a development from dynamite to nylon. By strange paradox, the women, not the men of the world, are the ultimate determinant of Du Pont policy. Much more than on dynamite, the company rests on housewives."

THERE'S A DIVINITY THAT SHAPES OUR ADS!

The November 17, 1923, cover of *Judge*, a humor magazine, featured a galaxy of feminine ads,† a tribute to the ladies' new role as purchasing agents for the American family.

Women were a major force in transforming autos. They wanted, and got, color, style, comforts, self-starters, automatic windshield wipers, and theft-proof locks for car wheels.

†Including the Misses Heinz, Holeproof, Fleisher, Venida, Mavis, Hinds, Gainsborough, Life Saver, Zip, Mulsified, Mum, Dorin, Coca Cola, and the Palm Olive and Luxite sisters.

FROM "TREASURY OF EARLY AMERICAN AUTOMOBILES" BY FLOYD CLYMER

Charles Evans Hughes was first presidential aspirant to use auto extensively for campaigning. Although both candidates spoke glowingly of U. S. resources, shortages were severe. Hughes' car depended on Malayan rubber, Mrs. Hughes' clothing on imported silk, dyes.

SCIENCE SAHARA

THE U. S. liked to boast, in the excitable era of World War I, that one American could lick any ten Germans that ever lived; such confident remarks were as much a part of the times as trench kits, collections of peach pits and "K-K-K-Katie." Sober minds saw, however, that in one respect the German soldier had enjoyed an advantage that could well nullify any kind of courage. Organic chemistry, creator of dyes, medicinals and a hundred other necessities, had for many years been a German industrial monopoly. Until this country could build up its own resources, its needs could be met only at the whim of a foreign power.

"Let's try it," said Irénée du Pont. "We ought to be as smart as the Germans."

For a time it didn't seem so. The job called for a brand of expert technology which existed nowhere in America. The complexities of organic chemistry were being explored in a few of the better colleges and scientific schools, but by fewer students than today take up Sanskrit or Greek. Americans who could carry a tricky and unpredictable organic process from the laboratory out into the factory and make it work were even more rare. There was no pool of talent on which to draw. As the wartime famine of good dyes, fine chemicals and modern pharmaceuticals had all too grimly proved, neither the industry nor the country was anywhere near self-sufficient. Novocaine, a routine item of the dentist's pharmacopoeia, had sold during the war for as much as $1600 a pound; it was a German product and only the Germans knew how to make it. Organic dyes of any quality were also largely German in origin; during the war the Far East was combed for leftover German dyes that were re-sold at fantastic prices. Only Europeans knew how to draw nitrogen out of the air on a commercial basis; America still got its nitrates for explosives and fertilizers from Chile. Iodine, silk and rubber had to come from abroad. Even in peacetime, iodine cost $5 a pound, silk cost whatever the Japanese chose to charge, the price of rubber could be pegged at will. Such things were irritating in peace, for they forced the country to pay a sort of ransom to attain the living standard it desired. And in war this dependence on foreign technology could well prove fatal.

Rubber, which U.S. had to import, came from Malaya, was a tight British monopoly; its price and supply fluctuated wildly.*

Silk was more unpredictable in supply and price than rubber. Japanese earthquake of 1923 panicked the U. S. silk market.

Ship sinkings and disasters affected U. S. imports, forced chemical industry to find ways to eliminate dependence on foreign goods.

*In one year, for instance, from 1924 to 1925, price of rubber rose from 26 cents to 72 cents, an increase of more than 280 per cent. Later, its price was arbitrarily pegged by the British at $1 a pound by the "Stevenson Cartel" Acts.

KNOW-HOW IS WHERE YOU FIND IT

IN building their country, Americans had turned many a stretch of grim wilderness into a populous and productive community. Du Pont now proposed to deal similarly with the Technological Desert then stunting the roots of industrial progress. In the next 20 years, the blossoming process was to call for the risk of $400,000,000, but it was to produce some interesting roses indeed.

In general, they grew from three basic seeds:

Some, like dyes and organic chemicals, had to be coaxed laboriously from hard and stony soil, with little background to guide the hand.

Some, like the "Duco" finish that was to revolutionize automobile-making, developed out of original research following earlier ventures in lacquer and paints.

Some, like ammonia, rayon and cellophane, resulted from buying the basic technology abroad, then improving on it after it had been transplanted to this country.

The venture in dyes was a dear one, but eventually it was as productive in experience as in output. Du Pont had plunged in, with little preparation, to find itself dealing with chemical reactions that were mere textbook references to the few home-grown chemists then available. A few processes were acquired from a British firm, and later some refugee German chemists, eager for asylum, joined the team. In 1918, seized German patents were purchased, but proved to be of only moderate aid. The Germans had had a habit of being less than candid in their disclosures; sometimes they revealed all but the essential element of a chemical formula; sometimes they mischievously added others that were tried with disagreeable consequences.

This trial-and-error process took time and money. Not until the Thirties was the dyestuffs venture to pay back its initial cost; the plant's location at Deepwater Point, N. J., was for a long time a wry joke financially.

In a negative sense, dyes emphasized the importance of background, just as "Duco" affirmed it positively. Until research experience could be built up on a broad scale, it would save time to import the needed know-how instead of the finished products.

Three purchases from Europe were to be of especially far-reaching importance. One was a French process for fixation of nitrogen. Later, when improved after much research, it helped relieve the country of dependence on Chilean nitrates through economic production of ammonia. Eventually it was also to help furnish basic materials for crystal-clear plastics and man-made fibers.*

Two other products were acquired from the French in the early Twenties, after negotiations led by Vice-president William C. Spruance. (For whom a rayon plant at Richmond is named.) One was rayon, then known as "artificial silk," and at first relegated by American women to off-stage utilitarian duties. The other was cellophane, then a luxury item selling for $2.65 a pound, unresistant to moisture, and of little actual use except as a decorative wrapping for expensive perfumes. Both had cellulose, so familiar to Du Pont, as a basic ingredient; both had serious handicaps to be overcome if they were ever to reach mass markets.

Much time, effort and money were to be required before these deficiencies were overcome. But eventually the program was successful; like other immigrants the new arrivals from abroad were to win far greater renown in America than they had in their native lands.

Meanwhile, the first major development of the earlier, cellulose-based technology had come to maturity. In a laboratory at Parlin, chemists had been working for years to find a quick-drying lacquer that would give greater thickness with fewer coats. Eventually, they were to find it and call it "Duco" pyroxylin lacquer. It was Du Pont's first All-American laboratory development, and it was soon to have an astonishing effect upon the American scene.

Edmond Gillet, head of French firm which owned rayon process, became a Du Pont director.

Jacques Brandenberger developed cellophane in France. Du Pont bought rights in 1923.

Dr. Marston Bogert of Columbia Univ. reported U. S. had no organic chemical industry.

Francis P. Garvan, as Alien Property Custodian, seized German chemical patents for U. S.

*Another important outgrowth was synthetic methanol, or wood alcohol, formerly made by distilling wood. In World War I it was scarce and costly; by World War II it was in great demand but the supply was adequate and the cost very low.

By 1925, Experimental Station's facilities and personnel had grown. Substantial technical progress could be reported, especially in cellulose products. But the nation's expanding needs required a broader scientific base than had yet been developed in the U. S.

At Belle, W. Va., in 1925 Du Pont built plant to make ammonia under high pressure. Process, acquired from French, was changed completely as Du Pont gained know-how. Venture represented investment of more than $27 million before profits offset losses.

Chambers Works marked Du Pont's entrance into field of organic chemistry. To help overcome dependence on foreign sources* for dyes and related chemicals, Du Pont invested $43,000,000 here before sufficient profits were earned to cancel accumulated losses.

*In 1916 the German submarine *Deutschland* ran British blockade to bring a load of dyes to U. S., which was running low on colors for postage stamps and currency. German dyes cartel that Du Pont was to beard had textile market under thumb: if customer bought one available dye elsewhere Germans would cut off supply of those on which they had monopoly.

SUMMER DRESS BULLETIN

Leading women's wear manufacturers note a greater demand for soft, cool rayon dresses this season than ever before

By R. H. FISHER

SUMMER dresses of rayon! That is fashion's word for warm weather attire. Everywhere on city streets and at the popular resorts rayon dresses appear—dresses of every hue, design and style.

This popularity is undoubtedly due to the fact that both dress manufacturers and dress wearers now fully recognize the exceptional quality of these rayon and rayon-mixed garments. Indeed, practically all of the leading dress goods manufacturers are using rayon in substantial quantities. It is being used particularly in combination with silk or cotton.

These rayon mixtures afford great opportunities for the exercise of creative individuality, and well-known dress stylists, realizing the possibilities offered in rayon dresses, have given special attention to developing new vogues and new styles to show the fabrics to best advantage.

Important dress manufacturers who are using these special rayon styles and fabrics have placed on the market striking models that have won instant popularity. Throughout the country department stores and women's wear shops have been quick to see the beauty of the new garments and have featured them prominently.

(Continued on page 14)

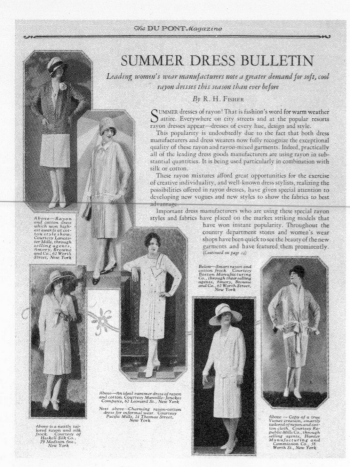

Above—Rayon and cotton dress which won highest awards at cotton style show. Courtesy Lancaster Mills, through selling agents, Amory, Browne and Co., 62 Worth Street, New York

Below—Smart rayon and cotton frock. Courtesy Boston Manufacturing Co., through their selling agents, Amory, Browne and Co., 62 Worth Street, New York

Above—An ideal summer dress of rayon and cotton. Courtesy Manville-Jenckes Company, 65 Leonard St., New York

Next above—Charming rayon-cotton dress for informal wear. Courtesy Pacific Mills, 24 Thomas Street, New York

Above is a neatly tailored rayon and silk frock. Courtesy of Haskell Silk Co., 79 Madison Ave., New York

Above — Copy of a true Vionet creation, smartly tailored of rayon and cotton cloth. Courtesy Republic Mills Co., through selling agents, Hunter Manufacturing and Commission Co., 58 Worth St., New York

Rayon, originally a cheap and often shoddy substitute for silk, was transformed by research and investment into a staple of feminine wardrobe. New dye colors increased variety of women's clothes.

Three of the seven popular models of the Oakland Line. Duco is the finishing material used on all models

1924 Oaklands Finished in Duco

Here's some more information about the finish that is adding to the well-deserved popularity of a truly fine car

By F. H. KANE
Technical Engineer
Oakland Motor Car Co.

AMONG the hundreds of automobiles displayed at the national automobile shows this year in New York and Chicago, one of the most interesting lines was the "True Blue Oakland," manufactured by the Oakland Motor Car Company, Pontiac, Michigan. These cars embody the latest and most approved engineering principles, including also many features not to be found on other cars, regardless of price. First among these improvements is the new du Pont automobile finish, Duco, which is now standard on the entire Oakland line.

The 1924 Oakland line includes seven models. The bodies, built by the Fisher Body Corporation, are substantial and businesslike, yet altogether pleasing in appearance. Among the mechanical features are the six-cylinder "L" head engine with a special combustion chamber in the cylinder head designed to produce a thorough mixture of gasoline and air, resulting in increased power.

Four-wheel brakes are standard on all Oakland models. A unique centralized control and all the instruments under glass on the instrument board are important innovations. The centralized control includes choker, throttle and horn buttons, lighting and ignition switches. These are all mounted on an aluminum housing in the center of the steering wheel. Incorporated in the lighting switch is a device which permits the

Right—Before applying the priming coats or Duco the car body must be clean. This shows you the metal "clean-up"

Below—This shows one of the huge drying ovens used to bake on the priming coats. You will note that it is wide enough to accommodate three car bodies and high enough for a full-grown man to stand under the hood without stooping

Below—Glazing the car body after the priming coats have been applied

"Duco" finishes, introduced in 1923, broke critical bottleneck in auto industry, when their quick-drying properties cut car-painting time from 26 days to 5 hours, shifted assembly lines into high gear.

"BRINGING HOME THE BACON"

How Cellophane literally carries out a well-known figure of speech

By A. W. SHAFFER

ABOUT three years ago a wide-awake meat packer saw in the glistening, transparent wrapper used on candy boxes the ideal means for protecting his sliced bacon when displayed on the dealer's counter. He recognized an additional and highly advantageous quality in that this wrapper permitted the attractiveness of his product to be instantly visualized by the prospective customer.

In this manner one of the most useful methods of marketing bacon and other dried and smoked meats was conceived. In the old days, when little thought was given to safeguarding health by strict protection of all foodstuffs from the dangers of contamination, bacon, if displayed at all, was displayed "in the open"—uncovered.

Later, when the importance of protection for foodstuffs became evident to health authorities, the packers adopted a package wrapper for their bacon and similar products. Although such protective wraps and packages generally solved the problem from the standpoint of contamination, they failed from the important merchandising standpoint of showing the goods to the best advantage, since such wrappings usually hid the contents completely.

In Cellophane, the packers found the means for providing both complete protection and perfect visibility and as a result, this absolutely sanitary and transparent material is used today on the millions of packages of bacon marketed by over two hundred packing companies. In the packing industry this interesting development of a transparent package has not been confined to bacon alone, for during the past year many companies have begun to wrap sausage, dried beef, frankfurters, bacon squares, ham butts, meat loaves and even whole hams in Cellophane.

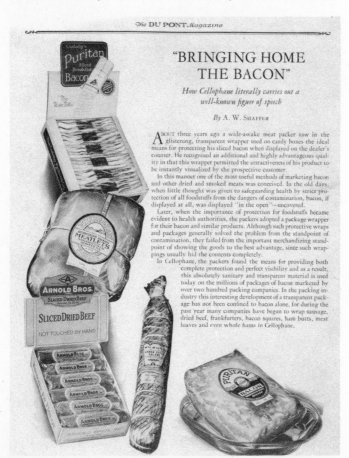

Moistureproof cellophane, developed in 1927, gave real utility to frilly French product, found enthusiastic markets in food and tobacco packaging. Technological improvements sharply cut its price.

And Now—du Pont Dials

The extensive use of Pyralin-made radio panels has stimulated the demand for dials to match—so here they are

By L. B. STEELE

A FEW months ago we told you about du Pont panels as a new use for Pyralin in radio sets. Since that announcement, these panels have gained wide favor and are now in use in thousands of sets throughout the country.

Their easy workability, their exceptionally fine appearance and unusual dielectric properties have made them a prime favorite among amateur set builders everywhere.

And now in response to a consistent demand for dials to match these panels, the Pyralin Department has placed on the market the du Pont dial. Exceptionally good-looking is this dial, with a luster which makes it far more attractive than those made of the usual dial materials. It is obtainable in either black or red mahogany effects—the latter a splendid simulation of grained wood.

All of the larger dials have a graduation scale attractively engraved, and the rheostat knobs have the usual arrow marker; see the one illustrated above. These markings show no tendency to rub off with constant handling. The dials are made in

The Pyralin rheostat knob

the following sizes: 5-inch diameter, 4-inch diameter, and 1¾-inch diameter.

Radio set manufacturers have been much impressed with the beauty of these new dials. The Garod Corporation, of Newark, New Jersey, an important manufacturer of radio sets, has used the mahogany-colored dials on its new Model V set which is illustrated here. These dials are in keeping with the exceptional beauty of this set which has met with such wide favor that the Garod Corporation's capacity has been taxed to fill orders.

If you wish to install dials of this type on the new set you are building, or to substitute them for the less-attractive dials on your old set—and many are doing that—then go to your local radio dealer and ask to see samples. If he doesn't carry them in stock, we suggest that you write to the Pyralin Department, E. I. du Pont de Nemours & Co., Inc., Arlington, New Jersey.

Right—The du Pont dial in large enough size to show the grain effect, but our picture gives only a hint of its beauty

Below—The Garod Neutrodyne needs no introduction to radio fans. Model V is shown, and it is equipped with du Pont dials

Plastics found an immediate outlet in many different industries. Radio makers used them on both inside and outside of their sets; auto industry adapted one to need for shatter-proof safety glass.

SHAPING NEW WAYS OF LIFE

THE U. S. family of 1900 lived in much the same way as the U. S. family of 1875. In sharp, vivid, exciting contrast, the U. S. family of 1925 was to live a life which 1900 would have regarded as utterly fantastic. And in few phases of this new design for living was Du Pont to play a bystander's role, as articles in the *Du Pont Magazine* (see opposite page) showed clearly.

Most conspicuous was the change brought about by the automobile. Once "Duco" topped the hurdle that had slowed production, the new cars reshaped social patterns as rapidly as they created traffic. (Registrations rose from 3 million to 20 million between 1918 and 1928.)* Suburban developments sprang up (many with alluring names like Wykliff Heights and Wuthering Manor). This was the simple effect of transportation: people no longer had to live close to their jobs. And no longer did they lunch at home, so that new restaurants, plant cafeterias and that peculiar institution, the drug store lunch counter, rose everywhere.

What happened was that technology had at last outstripped the necessities of the growing population, and was providing real dividends in better living. This was happening in laboratories, producing improvements in everything from rayon to gasolines. And it was happening in factories, where more efficient equipment and techniques were multiplying production and reducing hours of labor. It had been a miracle when Henry Ford turned out his first million cars in seven years; the tenth million took 132 days, with employees working far less time.

With added leisure, resulting from greater industrial output, came further changes. One was the motion picture; theaters doubled the number of seats for sale in 10 years. Both film and auto changed fashions; a lady kicking at a self-starter needed her skirt short; under the influence of Miss Clara Bow she wanted it bright and glamorous. With so many roads to explore, beaches to visit, radio programs to listen to, and stadia to jam, people appreciated easy living and easy shopping. They demanded food that could be prepared quickly; self-service and new cellophane wrappings proved popular.

The family vacation underwent sharp change; quick trips by auto, rather than extended pilgrimages, became the vogue. Week-end summer cottages (Uneeda Rest or Dew-Drop-In) sprang up on thousands of rivers and lakes, now that they were accessible by road. There was more money for parks and playgrounds, for recreation (golf courses spread everywhere) and, in a more sober vein, for hospitals and medical research. The rush to the country, plus the new school bus, brought the consolidated school, with facilities greatly beyond those of local communities.

Thoughtful men pondered these changes. Some deplored them, but most saw that higher living standards were essential to national progress. But American chemistry knew well that much still remained to be done. Late in the decade, Du Pont made a significant move toward this goal.

*Confounding the *Literary Digest*, which though a leading periodical of the times was to win small fame for accurate forecasting. Earlier it had announced that while use of the automobile would increase, it would never, *of course*, be as widespread as the bicycle. Those who worried, however, about increasing "materialism" often lost sight of broad cultural gains. Mid-Twenties saw great number of significant literary works, far exceeding earlier periods. Among them: *Arrowsmith, The Sun Also Rises, Manhattan Transfer, John Brown's Body, A Lost Lady, Look Homeward Angel.*

By 1924, wages of Du Pont employees were more than twice as high as in 1914, reflecting the company's expanded production. In same 10-year period, "real" wages jumped nearly 20 per cent.

Leisure-time activities increased as people had more time for themselves and more money to spend. Average hours of work per week in U. S. dropped from 60 in 1900 to 47 in 1930, were to fall more.

Educational opportunities were broadening and more young people, especially girls, were going on to college. College endowments, almost $1 billion in 1925, had more than doubled by 1951.

Six of the first group of scientists assigned to Du Pont's fundamental research program pose* under the chemical symbols for rubber, silk, cellulose and formaldehyde polymer. Though these chemists knew enough in 1927 to chart their structures, they did not understand how they were formed. To synthesize similar materials, they would have to probe an uncommunicative Nature.

*From left to right: George L. Dorough, Glen A. Jones, Julian W. Hill, James E. Kirby, Gerard J. Berchet, Frank J. Van Natta.

JOURNEY INTO THE UNKNOWN

IN a quiet room overlooking the famous Harvard Yard a young instructor in chemistry fingered a well-creased note bearing the letterhead of E. I. du Pont de Nemours and Co. It was 1927, and the 31-year-old Wallace Hume Carothers already had made a name for himself in the research field. Now, in an exchange of correspondence destined to become historic, there was placed before him a problem unlike any he had yet faced in his laboratory. For the Du Pont Company, a firm dedicated to profit, was proposing that he leave the academic world and take charge of a research program unusual to industry. Du Pont, wrote Dr. C. M. A. Stine, then director of the Chemical Department, was about to strike out into the field of basic science—the investigation of the fundamental secrets of matter. Would Dr. Carothers come and take charge of a group studying organic chemistry?* He would have such facilities, help and financial support as were seldom at the disposal of a college scientist.

Dr. Wallace Carothers, a promising young chemist, headed fundamental program in organic chemistry.

For a time, Dr. Carothers hesitated. The field described was, at the time, of interest mainly to colleges and to endowed bodies unconcerned with profit. Carothers had his doubts, but Dr. Stine was persuasive. In a brief, laconic scrawl, the young scientist agreed to come. Thus, under Dr. Stine's direction, was Du Pont's venture into fundamental research launched. It was a program which soon was to have far-reaching results.

In embarking on such a risky voyage (fundamental research is the longest-range kind of scientific venture) Du Pont had no thought of supplanting or competing with similar work being done by the universities. The academic world, it well knew, provided the atmosphere in which the search for basic truth and new knowledge could flourish most effectively. Du Pont undertook these investigations in fields of present or potential interest since the universities could not be expected to do all the necessary research in these areas.

The relationship between pure and applied research had drawn much discussion since the nation's start.

Franklin, Paine, Jefferson and Pierre Samuel du Pont had been interested in the problem. A French visitor who wrote a notable book about the U. S. in the 1840's commented on American business' sense of urgency, and expressed doubt that it could ever produce much in the way of theoretical or abstract conclusions. "Nothing is more necessary," wrote Alexis de Tocqueville, "to the culture of the higher sciences than meditation, and nothing is less suited to meditation than the structure of democratic society." The temptation to produce something for ready sale would, he felt, obscure any long-range objectives.

In their new laboratory on the Brandywine, Dr. Carothers and his group of picked men were provided with an environment designed to isolate them from the distractions of immediate operating problems. There were no strings attached. The men were free to choose their own projects and to carry out their research along lines that seemed most desirable. Their destination, it turned out, was a previously unexplored kingdom, far beyond microscope range, in which molecules a millionth of an inch long were classified as "giants." These were the mysterious building blocks from which Nature had created rubber, silk and other materials, and which were still well-guarded secrets after centuries of guesswork by scientists. It was a program that was to require years of work and study; it is still going forward under a group of outstanding Ph.D.'s in Du Pont laboratories. By no means, however, is the fundamental field the exclusive province of the Chemical Department. All research divisions were eventually to participate in pioneering. Even construction materials and machine design came in for this type of study. It was recognized that the cost would be high and the route long and twisting; in choosing difficult problems, Du Pont commits itself to long, patient investigations in which the horizons continually recede. But overall, fundamental research, in university and industrial laboratories alike, would enable chemistry to meet Nature on her own grounds—those of sheer creative virtuosity.

ARCHIMEDES   **DE TOCQUEVILLE**

U. S. industry was to dispute Archimedes' view that useful end for science was "low, mercenary and vile." De Tocqueville, in 1840, had noted America's preoccupation with practical aims.

*Other groups were assigned to fundamental studies in such fields as physics, physical chemistry and colloid chemistry.

DEPRESSION

Stock market crash on "Black Friday" in October, 1929 brought gloom to Wall Street, above, set off the Depression. Du Pont stock slid from 231 to 80. Dividend dropped from $4.00 to $2.75 in '32.

FEW adult Americans need to be told that in October of 1929 a panic on the stock market was followed by what was, to them at least, the most gruelling economic depression the nation had ever experienced. Industrial output slowed from a gallop to a walk; big and small businesses alike were affected; farm prices slumped and cities had to cope with problems of relief.

Almost as numerous as the tragedies were the theories as to just what had caused it. One favorite explanation was the "bust" of the long and frenzied "boom" market that had bloated the prices of many securities far beyond any recognizable connection with the value of the assets they represented. Another pet explanation was "over-production"; so, incidentally, was "under-production."

Presently, however, an important fact about the situation began to emerge more and more clearly. At the start of the crash, the American living standard had been higher than ever before in the country's history—so high that much of the average family's income had been going into what might be called "deferrable items." These were things beyond the basic necessities of food, clothing and shelter that were pleasant but not necessary to buy: automobiles, radios, mechanical iceboxes, and so on. The eager purchase of such things—and there were hundreds of them—had helped make the "boom"; the sudden slow-down created unemployment in factories and stores.

Du Pont, though hit along with the rest of industry, took a bold course. Though ten millions, at one time, were said to be unemployed, the fact remained that forty-odd millions were still very much employed. Du Pont management, looking at the long term, felt that normal times would come back only if industry continued its research, opened new plants, and went on developing new products, thus creating new jobs and opportunities. As against the policy of "let's wait this thing out," this was the constructive, dynamic approach. Du Pont was not to be long in choosing.

Hard times forced people to look for cheap pleasures near home. Miniature golf boomed, as did dance marathons, jigsaw puzzles.

Unemployment topped 10 million in 1932. Du Pont was hit, but new construction and developments and spreading of work held lay-offs to minimum. Total employment declined in only three years.

Company research went on, prodded by Lammot du Pont, who said "it is more important . . . than dividends."

"ENTERPRISE AND COURAGE"

DU PONT'S Annual Report of 1931 acknowledged that the U.S. was undergoing "no ordinary depression." But it had a prophetic word of hope: "The stimulus of our wants, combined with the energy and capacity of the American people, will gradually bring back a prosperity based on real values and an abandonment of unsound speculative dreams."

Rock bottom, as recorded by the financial seismograph, was reached in July, 1932. The Annual Report for 1932 confirmed this fact, noting a "better than seasonal" upswing in the second half of the year. Though there was uncertainty as to what was described as "the synthetic route" to prosperity, "there have appeared no ailments," Lammot du Pont reported, "which may not be expected to yield to patience, enterprise and courage."

Taking this word literally, Du Pont started out to give a living example.

In '30's, company continued policy of growth and expansion. Investment doubled, employment rose by 6500.

Six Depression Babies

Neoprene, first commercially successful* synthetic rubber and fruit of fundamental research, is shown by Wallace Carothers.

Refrigerators were improved by new products: "Dulux" synthetic resin enamels in 1930; "Freon" safe refrigerant in 1930.

Insecticides represented entirely new field of Du Pont endeavor, which was to lead to broad interest in agricultural chemicals.

Acetate, which the company began making in 1929, added beauty to high fashion apparel, and meant jobs for thousands.

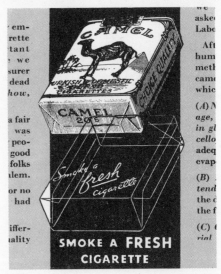

Moistureproof cellophane boomed for cigarette wrappings. From 1929 to 1932, sales increased 5 times, price was halved.

"Lucite" acrylic resin symbolized new age of plastics, was glamorized in a film starring David Niven and Loretta Young.

*Announced in 1931, it found immediate acceptance even at its price of $1.05 a pound. Ten years later, vastly improved, it sold for 65 cents a pound.

BUSINESS TO BLAME

"WHEN the manger is empty," runs an old saying. "the horses bite each other." People made panicky by economic depression often act much the same way: a scapegoat is selected, blame for the whole difficulty transferred to his unfortunate shoulders. The depression being world-wide, this process began all over the world. In Germany and Italy a variety of villains was named, and men of Hitler's and Mussolini's stripe were pleased to administer retribution. In the U. S., the scapegoat nominated was simply business.

Thus business, in the thick of its struggle to help the nation back on its economic feet, at the same time was obliged to endure a barrage of official censure. Even honesty and patriotism were questioned; bankers and financiers were attacked as a group. Business leaders appeared before unfriendly Congressional committees. And Du Pont, praised a few years before as a bulwark of civilization when its munitions were stemming the German tide, was haled before a Senate Committee. It was headed by Gerald P. Nye, a North Dakota Republican whose banner was flung high with the cry of "Merchants of Death." The hearings were inconclusive and often futile, but they left their stamp on public consciousness.

New laws were established. Some were good, but many limited the operation of enterprise. And some would have to be scrapped hastily a few years hence when once again the world was to need, desperately, the full productive strength of American industry.

The Blue Eagle symbolized NRA, which established a new relationship between business and the Government. Up to now the Government had played a passive role.

Decade Before the Deluge

Hitler came to power in Germany in 1933, armed for aggression that sparked a global war.

Mussolini's Italian trains ran on time, but his craze for power drove him to war and ruin.

Japan's aggressions, culminating at Pearl Harbor, began with 1932 invasion of Manchuria.

In Spain, Franco began Civil War which became prelude to fight between fascism and free world.

Facing Nye Committee at 1934 open hearing are Irénée du Pont (with pipe), Pierre S. du Pont and Lammot du Pont. Committee's theme was that "munitions making" was a social wrong, but company had no apologies for filling wartime needs of armed forces.*

TRIAL
WITHOUT
JURY

Nye Committee, l. to r.: Senators Vandenberg, Barbour, Nye; Alger Hiss, legal assistant; Senator Clark; Stephen Raushenbush, chief investigator; Senator Pope. Vandenberg and Barbour disagreed with colleagues.

A Senate committee investigating utility practices was headed by Senator Hugo Black, second from left, now on the Supreme Court.

J. P. Morgan, standing right, led a long list of banking and financial leaders who testified in Senate probe of Wall Street activity.

*Walter S. Carpenter, Jr., in light suit, sits behind Irénée du Pont. Other Du Pont witnesses present were K. K. V. Casey, Dr. Fin Sparre, A. Felix du Pont. Irénée du Pont's disarming candor won wide approval with public and press.

103

New construction, like this large rayon and cellophane plant built by Du Pont at Richmond, Va., laid basis for long-range progress.

New industries like air conditioning appeared. Sound pictures and radio grew rapidly, setting new standards of mass entertainment.

SIGNALS AHEAD: THIS WAY OUT

MINIATURE golf lasted only one brief summer and a song called "Brother Can You Spare a Dime" little longer. The way out of the depression, clearly, lay in revitalizing the economy through creation of new jobs and new opportunities. Temporary measures, though relieving immediate need, offered no long-term solution. As the pictures here indicate, industry generally shared Du Pont's view of the constructive approach. Soon sights were raised; not the standards of 1929 but new levels, far beyond, became the goal.

To reach this inviting plateau required far more than

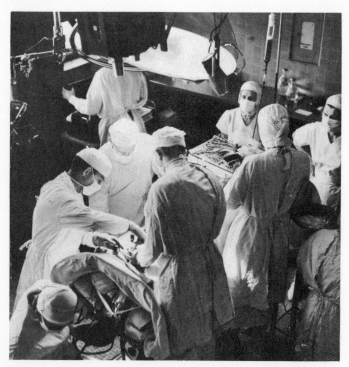

New discoveries* paced growth of the drug industry. Today, 80 per cent of prescriptions call for drugs unknown 20 years ago.

Supermarkets carried benefits of mass distribution into grocery basket. Frozen foods came in, adding variety to American menus.

*Materials for the first U. S. sulfa drugs were made in Du Pont's Chambers Works.

Lower prices and improved efficiency of farm machinery led to greater mechanization which upped U. S. farm output 9 per cent.

Electric power, accurate gauge of U. S. industrial growth, increased from 91 billion kilowatt hours in 1930 to 127 billion in 1939.

brave talk or shows of confidence. (Like the club whose members wore badges announcing that the slump would end at 3 P. M.) More tangible means were required: the courageous venture of millions of dollars. From 1930 to 1936 alone, Du Pont was to put more than $160 million into new chemical products. At the same time, it affirmed its faith in expansion and productivity by adding new activities: in 1930 Roessler & Hasslacher (electrochemicals, sodium, ceramic colors and peroxides) joined Du Pont;* and in 1931 came the important titanium pigments.

But coming into the chemical field was another develop-

ment, destined to rank in importance with mass production—the continuous-flow plant, operating around both clock and calendar. Continuous process was to revolutionize living habits of towns and cities through shift schedules and staggered week-ends, but by lowering costs it produced something further: new business opportunities. (In one direction alone, production of low-cost plastic materials has bred 4000 fabricators of plastic products since 1930, with an annual business of over $250 million.) Here indeed was the way out, and through such methods, endlessly repeated, was the nation to recover and reach new peaks.

Oil refineries expanded from wider use of autos, diesel engines, home burners. Oil output jumped 50 per cent from 1930 to 1940.

Improved technology led to expansion of Belle plant in 1932. Industry invested $13 billion in plants, equipment from 1930-1939.

*Just as had, in 1928, the Grasselli Chemical Co., an old and distinguished producer of heavy chemicals and insecticides.

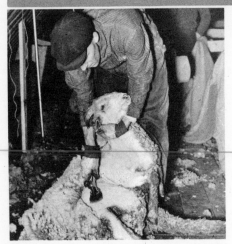

Animals such as sheep and goats provide a substantial portion of the world's fibers.

Vegetable source, such as cotton, is largest, but the weather affects its price and supply.

Forest provides wood pulp whose cellulose is principal raw material for rayon, first man-made fiber.

NYLON

Nylon was first spun mechanically on this crude machine. For a spinneret, researchers used a drug store hypodermic needle.

ON September 21, 1938, the nation's press reported issue of a patent covering a new textile fiber which was described, with enthusiasm, as "a new silk, made on a chemical base." Within a few months all the world was to know the story and the product's name: nylon.

The best-known outgrowth of the company's research progress, nylon for many reasons is one of the most important developments in Du Pont's long history:

It was the world's first fiber comparable to Nature's fibers, the climax of centuries of search.

It was in the first rank of American discoveries—the fruit of the chemical industry's first large-scale fundamental research program.

It struck another critical item from the list of materials for which the U.S. was dependent on foreign sources.

It became the gossamer and glamor in milady's wardrobe, yet strong and tough in a thousand industrial articles.

It was the first of a whole new family of synthetics to bring new beauties, economies and conveniences to the American consumer.

It became, world-wide, a symbol of the abundance and comfort and luxury of U. S. life today.

The chemical product that is all these things was the result of a concept born in the minds of Dr. Carothers and his associates 10 years earlier. Laboratories and pilot plants created the technology necessary to its development, and it was brought to commercial production in record time at an expensive, intricate new plant at Seaford, Delaware.

The formative stage was precarious. Hosiery was a promising field, but early experiments were discouraging. The first pair of nylon stockings made (now stored in the company's Hall of Records) drew sniffs from a merchandising expert called in to examine them. Test after test was made to determine the stresses and strains an active lady's legs put upon her hosiery.

Du Pont secretaries became guinea pigs. So did dancers, like the famed Rockettes. Difficulties were soon overcome; the guinea pigs gave delighted squeals. Nylon was ready for market.

Legend, today, is the story of its sharp impact on the American scene. When the first women's hosiery of nylon went on sale, ladies frequently indulged in unladylike aggression in their determination to acquire a pair. U.S. women bought 64 million pairs in the first year, demanded more.

Less spectacular, but perhaps more significant, was what nylon meant to the hosiery manufacturer. Wildly fluctuating silk markets had him against the wall. Japan's monopoly of silk was absolute; the Nipponese used its thin strands to finance their aggression. Hosiery makers, confused and confounded by a product that might cost $1.50 a pound one day and, without any apparent reason, $3 a week later, turned eagerly to nylon. It presaged a stability in supply, quality and price that would allow them to

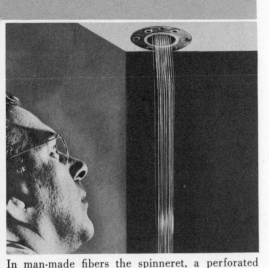

In man-made fibers the spinneret, a perforated disc, shapes molten mass into filaments for yarn.

operate their small businesses on a rational basis.

Nylon hosiery yarn was introduced at $4.27 a pound; silk was then $2.79. Clearly nylon had to offer something extra to challenge silk's strong position. It did: longer wear per unit of sheerness—a quality dear to the feminine heart.

Demand soon outdistanced supply. Seaford was not yet a year old when a second yarn plant was begun. Other Du Pont plants, making the materials from which yarn was spun, expanded. Each Du Pont addition created hundreds of new jobs within the company, plus thousands in the firms, large and small, which bought the yarn and converted it into useful products. Thus nylon followed a pattern familiar in the nation's industry: a large company invents and produces economically a new material; small firms—converters, dyers, retail stores—each add a service and gain a profit in making and distributing a finished article; and the consumer benefits most of all through a better value for her budget dollar.

No other major chemical development had the spontaneous reception accorded nylon. Rayon, invented in 1884, was a half a century gaining popular acceptance. Plastics were nearly as long. Nylon, in one leap, brushed aside the competition of silk (long dominant in the hosiery field) and soon was on its way to uses varying from machine bearings to ropes for tugboats.

Nylon, by all standards, was a prize!

$27,000,000 was invested by Du Pont in nylon over 13 years before getting into satisfactory commercial production. Fruit of the company's fundamental research program, nylon's debut climaxed the years of work by hundreds of Du Pont chemists and engineers. The fiber had to be scaled up from test tube to pilot plant; then commercial units were built at Belle, W. Va., for intermediates, and Seaford, Del., above, for yarn. Such a job can be achieved only by a firm with large resources.

TO SEE WHAT THIS MEANS TO EVERYDAY LIFE, TURN THE PAGE →

continued on next page 107

Betty Grable helped World War II bond sales by auctioning off her hose for $40,000.

HOW NYLON HIT THE U.S.

NYLON, as no other product since the horseless carriage, was to become a part of the lore and legend of America. Financial pages used it as a barometer of national production. Cartoonists and lyricists embraced and glorified it. Stars of stage and screen glamorized its name. Foreigners envied it as a mark of American abundance. Traders, during war shortages, found it a better item of barter than cigarettes or chocolate. Other products were given names designed to borrow on nylon's fame. In short, it joined peanuts, automobiles, hot dogs and baseball as a U. S. institution.

BY PERMISSION COPR. 1940, THE NEW YORKER MAGAZINE, INC.

10 CENTS is what Du Pont receives for the nylon yarn in a pair of ladies' hose. The rest of the purchase price pays for the contributions of throwsters, knitters, seamsters, dyers and retailers who make and sell the finished stocking. Because nylon's longer life reduced the average woman's hosiery budget, the savings became available to her and her family for the purchase of additional things. In this way, nylon and other products of industry have continually raised living standards to new heights.

FOR THE BACKGROUND OF THIS AGREEABLE SCENE, TURN THE PAGE ◄

Giant leg, 35 feet high, advertises nylons to the countryside surrounding Los Angeles.

Broadway show, "Early To Bed," in 1942 had song: *When the Nylons Bloom Again.*

New methods of hosiery merchandising, like slot machines, developed with nylon.

Hundreds of women formed a line a block long when a New York City store advertised a sale of the first post-war nylons. The long "nylon lines" wound their way through city streets across the U. S.

"Hawkins, step in here and show the guests your new nylon stockings!"

"Nylon!"

BY PERMISSION COPR. 1940, THE NEW YORKER MAGAZINE, INC.

"AM I HURTING YOU?"

NYLON

SILK HOSIERY

True enough today, but will the roles be reversed five years from now?

LULL BEFORE
THE STORM

Du Pont Exhibit at World's Fair was sub-titled "The Wonder World of Chemistry," featured demonstrations of the chemist's achievements.

IN the summer of 1939, red geraniums by the thousands lined the streets of Flushing Meadow Park where the City of New York, turned entrepreneur, was entertaining with a giant World's Fair. It was a hopeful presentation headlined the World of Tomorrow and American industry, on parade, revealed hopeful promise indeed.

Visitors to the Du Pont Exhibit (there were five million of them, that summer) saw the new nylon hosiery on living models, heard tales of promising new plastics and chemicals that would lighten the burdens and ease the discomforts of mankind. There were minor crises: the entomologist faced a shortage of Japanese beetles; the chemically-dressed lady sustained an awesome run in her stocking; and a practical joker substituted a bar of rock candy for the unbreakable plastic. But the show was received with enthusiasm; viewers left the grounds eager with anticipation of glorious wonders to come.

There was gaiety that summer, too. Strolling musicians played "Chattanooga Choo Choo" and "My Heart Belongs to Daddy." On the New York stage, critics endorsed "Life With Father" and "The Straw Hat Revue," with two youngsters named Danny Kaye and Imogene Coca. At the Fair, Miss Eleanor Holm led a bevy of swimming beauties in a show called the Aquacade, staged by Mr. Billy Rose. A young man later to become famous as Gregory Peck pushed visitors about in a boardwalk rolling chair.

Yet a certain uneasiness underlay the facade of optimism. Visitors welcomed at the Polish exhibit had to pass an unfinished structure which was to have noted the scenic attractions of Czechoslovakia. The building, symbolically, was dark and shuttered. At the Finnish Building, tourists could get a reindeer-meat sandwich, and if they craned their necks out the window could see the tower of the garish display which hymned the glories of the Union of Soviet Socialist Republics. Fascist Italy's building featured a giant waterfall, which brightened the view of those dining expensively on the terrace of the French Pavilion. Dark, slant-eyed little men from the Japanese Gardens strolled about. (They seemed fascinated by the nylon show at the Du Pont Exhibit.) Mr. Grover Whalen welcomed, with suitable pomp, the King and Queen of England.

On the last Sunday in August, a million people came to the Fair. There was much laughter and song, and the fireworks display over the Lagoon was particularly spectacular. Yet that vague, unspoken, electric tension hung in the air like an impending thunderstorm, ominous in its very stillness.

On September 1, a former Austrian drill corporal sent his Panzer Divisions across the Polish frontier and put an end to all that. The way of life of nearly everyone in the world was to feel the change, almost at once. Before long youngsters aiming at plaster ducks in the shooting galleries would bear heavier arms; before long the American industry that was hopefully planning for the multitudes would be diverted to a grimmer, more urgent assignment.

GLOBAL WAR
1939-1945

ARSENAL OF DEMOCRACY

I N November, 1939, people were already beginning to talk about the "Bore War." Germany had disposed of Poland and though Britain and France had declared war, all belligerents were marking time. But *H.M.S. Royal Oak* had been torpedoed in Scapa Flow, and the German battleship *Graf Spee* was in the South Atlantic.

Britain, undeceived, was preparing for the worst. In November a purchasing mission came to Wilmington and asked the company to build a smokeless powder plant to supply the mobilizing Empire forces.† There were delays and changes of plan; not until June 10, 1940, six months after estimates were submitted, was a contract signed. (This was one week after Dunkirk had been evacuated; one month to the day before the Nazi bombing of Britain began.)

From this day on, for more than five years, Du Pont (and its affiliate, Remington Arms) was to devote the bulk of its time, energies and facilities to providing materials needed for the security of the U. S., which quickly aligned itself with Britain's cause. As assignment was piled on assignment, it became clear that the company was to undertake its largest, most exacting, and most imperative task.

The American chemical industry had come a long way since World War I. It was turning out products that reached into every corner of American life—fibers for fabrics, finishes, plastics, medicines, vitamins and so on by the hundreds. Chemistry had, in a word, learned to produce both quantitatively and creatively. In view of the critical jobs at hand, it was a good thing for the U. S. that it had done so.

An important fact about the industry, however, was that the creation of new products takes time—usually many years. Research programs cannot produce overnight, no matter how urgent the need. Moreover, there was no question of "converting" as in the case of the heavy industries. Automobile factories can be changed over to jeeps, tanks or planes, but a neoprene plant produces only neoprene; nylon only nylon. The use, not the product itself, changes; supply becomes the critical factor.

To have a strong chemical industry in war is a national necessity. It was now to be proved that the only way to have one in time of war is to have one in time of peace.

Remington Arms Co., a Du Pont affiliate, produced at peak 25,000,000 cartridges a day. Some 450 Du Pont technicians and supervisors joined the Remington staff.*

Neoprene, only non-metal on Government's first "most critical" list, was made in Louisville, where company built new plant, turned it over to Government in 1942.

"Cordura" rayon for bomber tires (shown above with Du Pont workers) and for heavy duty military truck tires, at one point in war was at top of U. S. priority list.

*In addition to its own facilities, Remington operated five small arms ammunition plants for the Government. One, at Salt Lake City, was built by Du Pont's Engineering Department; the others under Remington supervision. Along with ammunition, Remington produced over a million rifles for Army Ordnance and did much research and development work of the highest importance. Good example: incendiary ammunition.

†This plant, built at Memphis, Tenn., was taken over subsequently by the U.S. Government and operated as the Chickasaw Ordnance Works.

1941

1942

BUILDING
THE PLANTS

THIS astonishing transformation, in pictures made from same West Virginia hillside, reveals how the Du Pont-built Morgantown Ordnance Plant came into being. It was repeated often in World War II; Du Pont's Engineering Dept. built for the Government 54 plants of various sizes at 32 locations, ranging from the $350,000,000 Hanford unit to small plant additions. Total cost: $1,034,000,000. Total fee, after taxes and all applicable charges: 1/15 of one per cent of the construction cost.

FIRST GOVERNMENT SMOKELESS POWDER PLANT, THE WORLD'S LARGEST, WAS BUILT BY 28,000 DU PONT WORKERS IN

A TON A
MINUTE

ALTHOUGH military explosives pre-war were less than two per cent of its activity, Du Pont produced between December, 1940, and August, 1945, a greater volume of smokeless powder and TNT than had ever before been produced by one organization, anywhere. At peak capacity the volume of smokeless powder rose to a ton per minute. A huge organization was rapidly recruited from other sections of the company to help activate the emergency program.* (Departments unconcerned with explosives-making loaned 1580 supervisory and technical personnel.)

Around small nucleus of 400 explosives workers in own plants Du Pont built a giant production program employing 37,000. First of 128 "E" awards is being presented here to Carney's Point plant.

Speed of program was evidenced when Major R. E. Hardy and John F. Daley, then manager of Indiana Ordnance Works, helped pack the big plant's first powder, 248 days after breaking ground.

*Engineering work on a second nylon yarn plant was given to an outside firm so Du Pont engineers could immediately concentrate on the emergency program.

INDIANA. IT PRODUCED MORE THAN A BILLION POUNDS, ALMOST AS MUCH AS DU PONT'S TOTAL WORLD WAR I OUTPUT.

Total production came to some 4,500,000,000 pounds of explosives (including 2,500,000,000 pounds of smokeless powder, 1,500,000,000 of TNT)—three times the huge World War I output, and 20 per cent above the entire volume used by all the Allies in the earlier war. The bulk was made in company-built, Government-owned plants.

At their peak, over 75,000 people were engaged in building and operations; the enlistment and training of so large a group was in itself a considerable task. Some 840,000 persons were finger-printed to screen out unsuitable individuals. Purchase of materials for the program reached the stupendous total of $2,000,000,000 in equipment and supplies, ranging from castor oil to turbo-generators.

One of the most vital achievements was in upping production far beyond expected capacity. In smokeless powder output, improved rates of production made it possible to abandon plans for additional plant facilities. Savings were notable; in money: nearly $200,000,000; in manpower: 40,000 men in a crowded labor market; in time: 12 months whose value could be assessed only in human lives.

Powder flows from car into hopper which leads to conveyor belt. Improved equipment such as this helped boost daily powder line output 50 per cent. Biggest gains came through better methods.

Du Pont established new safety records during World War II. Accident rate averaged 1.44 per million man-hours worked, compared to 10.0 for chemical industry and 14.0 for all U.S. industry.

Hanford Engineer Works, where plutonium was first produced, covered 600 square miles in Washington, was first to mass-produce this fissionable material. Du Pont built and operated it at Government's request. Area shown is one of the eight operating units.

Town of Richland, Wash., was virtually built from the ground* up to house the 3275 Du Pont families who were transferred to project, and thousands recruited from outside the company. The bustling town was a modern, complete, self-sufficient community.

*Mostly sage brush and desert land.

ATOMIC ENERGY

Historic photograph shows men prominent in the development of atomic energy and the bomb it powered as they gathered in 1946 to honor Dr. Arthur Compton on his inauguration as Chancellor of Washington University in St. Louis. Seated, from left: Lt. Gen. Leslie Groves, Dr. Vannevar Bush, Dr. Enrico Fermi, Maj. Gen. Kenneth Nichols, Dr. George Pegram, Dr. Lyman Briggs. Standing, from left: Dr. Charles Thomas, Dr. James B. Conant, Chancellor Compton, Dr. Eger V. Murphree, Crawford H. Greenewalt.

EARLY in 1943, people in Du Pont's Wilmington headquarters, already occupied heavily with war work, became aware that something extra-special was going on. This promising chemist or that production specialist, it would be announced, was being transferred elsewhere, and he would depart at once for an unnamed destination. The terse name "TNX" was given the mystery project and literally hundreds of top people were to disappear into its dark anonymity.

In December of the preceding year, one Du Pont employee had joined a small group of scientists under the stands of a football stadium in Chicago and witnessed the first sustained chain reaction in an atomic pile. There was considerable doubt in his mind, he confessed later, as to whether either he, Crawford H. Greenewalt, or the city of Chicago, would survive the experiment.

This, then, was TNX, but until the closing months of 1945 only a handful of people would know the whole story behind the war's best-kept secret. Du Pont's part began late in 1942 when General Leslie R. Groves, head of the deadpan Manhattan Project, asked the company, in deepest confidence, to build and operate a plant for mass-production of a material then available only in a laboratory state. Less than a milligram of plutonium was in existence; it figured out to about 1/28,000th of an ounce.

Groves' errand was urgent. It was feared that the Germans were at work on atomic energy; getting there first could easily spell the difference between victory and disaster. Du Pont, unable to tell the whole story even to its top-level people, accepted, with two conditions: It would do the work for a fee of $1, and any patent rights would go to the Government. The company's venture into this strange and unknown field was launched, under the leadership of the late E. B. Yancey, then head of the Explosives Department, and of Roger Williams. (Later

Yancey and Williams became Du Pont vice-presidents.)

The task imposed wholly new problems. There were no precedents, no guideposts, no experience. Equipment never before imagined had to be designed and built. On top of everything else was the task of recruiting 45,000 workers, and transporting them and their families hundreds of miles to the plant site—where their new assignments were a complete secret.[*]

How big a job it was came to light only after Hiroshima, when the security curtain was partially lifted.

The plants built at the "Hanford Engineer Works" were huge and complex. They handled enormous quantities of materials through many successive processes with no human eye seeing — and few human brains knowing — what was going on. A complicated series of instruments, devised from scratch by Du Pont engineers, guided the flow by remote controls.

After the war, Du Pont prepared to relinquish its assignment to a more logical peacetime operator. (That Du Pont would, a few years hence, be called upon for an even greater atomic role then seemed remote as the moon.) There was the satisfaction that had come from meeting a difficult and exacting task. But it was the U. S. War Department that described the Hanford project as "a story of industrial energy, action, sacrifice, high morale." And General Groves noted that the Hanford task could not have succeeded without the contributions of Du Pont men—at all levels and stages of the mammoth pioneering exploit.

[*]An unverified legend of the plant involves a visit by a Senate committee investigating the war effort. Firmly denied entry, so the story goes, one Senator demanded of a guard, "What are they making in there?" Said the guard, without a qualm: "Bubble gum."

Anti-freeze, large part of which was diverted from civilian market, went into planes, tanks, military vehicles.

Cellophane protected and wrapped rations, drugs, ammunition, tank and plane parts, other vital equipment.

DDT protected troops and prisoners. Output was 4468 pounds in Nov., 1943. Total by war's end: 11,250,000.

Titanium was diverted from whitening agent in house paints to use in welding rods for ship-a-day program.

Tetraethyl lead was vital to aviation grade gasoline for air war, is credited with winning the Battle of Britain.

Nylon was taken off civilian market, went to war in parachutes, combat clothes and hundreds of other uses.*

Paints were used to protect equipment. It took thousands of gallons to cover a ship like *Missouri*, above.

"Lucite" acrylic resin output rate was upped to 4,500,000 square feet by 1945, made clear plane enclosures.

SWORDS AND PLOWSHARES

DU PONT'S wide diversification was reflected in the variety of goods and services it supplied during the emergency period. Materials from Du Pont operations ranged from chemicals used in heavy armament to such homely necessities as household cement. Government agencies as diverse as the Air Forces Technical Service and the Bureau of Printing and Engraving called for cooperation. Du Pont technology was addressed to incendiary bombs and to shoe soles. Not only military, but essential civilian needs had to be filled.

Such widely-separated activities were representative of the chemical industry's growth and advancement between the two wars.

In contrast to World War I, when explosives made up approximately 85 per cent of the Du Pont effort, military explosives accounted for less than 25 per cent of the company's total production in World War II. The fact that explosives production, although sharply reduced relatively, was still several times that of the previous war emphasized the shift. (See cuts.)

Du Pont was proud to perform a national service. But again it was to find that war is a losing game. Although business volume soars in wartime, higher tax rates, both immediate and long-term, impose harsh penalties. During World War II, earnings fell 21 per cent below the 1939-1941 average, and were even 5 per cent under the low average of 1936-1938.†

There was no profit, moneywise or otherwise, in war. Happily, peace was, once again, at hand.

WORLD WAR II
SOME DU PONT COMMERCIAL PRODUCTS

38,602,747 YARDS OF NYLON PARACHUTE YARN
Enough for 3,860,275 24-foot pack 'chutes.

80,000,000 SQUARE YARDS OF COATED FABRICS
More than enough to blanket all of Manhattan Island.

168,215,289 POUNDS OF "CORDURA" TIRE CORD
Enough for 14,017,940 heavy duty truck tires.

13,120,919 POUNDS OF NYLON TIRE CORD
Enough for 504,650 medium bomber tires.

268,904.545 LINEAR FEET OF 35 MM. MOTION PICTURE FILM
Or 50,929 miles.

92,900,000 POUNDS OF CELLOPHANE
Enough to make a strip 10 feet wide, extending from earth to moon.

40,000,000 GALLONS OF FINISHES
Enough to coat a 5½-foot fence circling the world at the equator.

26,153,000 POUNDS OF "LUCITE" ACRYLIC RESIN SHEETING
Enough for 370,000 bomber noses and gun turrets.

17,008,294 SQUARE FEET OF X-RAY FILM
Enough to make more than 30,000,000 8" x 10" medical X-ray negatives.

40,000,000 POUNDS OF VAT DYES
Enough to dye 1,770,000,000 linear yards of uniform cloth one yard wide.

---

*With nylon absorbed in the war effort and silk non-existent, tons of rayon were allocated to ladies' hosiery. Both ladies and connoisseurs of such matters recall this period with distaste.

†On the basis of present shares, 1939-1941 earnings averaged $1.87 per share of common stock, and in 1942-1945 fell to $1.48. In 1946, first post-war year, they rose to $2.36. Dividends paralleled this course.

POST-WAR EXPANSION

As U. S. returned to peace, last man left last of seven Government explosives plants which 37,000 Du Pont men and women had operated. He was H.E. Jackel of Wabash River (Ind.) Ordnance Works.

EACH Wednesday in the months following Japan's surrender in 1945 was an exciting day on the ninth floor of the Du Pont Building in Wilmington. For the company's Executive Committee, sitting there in its regular weekly meeting, was planning a long-term program of plant expansion and improvement on which, in just five years, Du Pont was to spend more than half a billion dollars.

During the war, the company's "normal" progress and development had stopped. Laboratories, their staffs scattered to war projects, limited their experiments almost exclusively to military or essential civilian projects. New plant construction was deferred because of concentration on the war effort and restricted materials. New products, unless they were vital, had to wait.

But post-war America had new needs and made new demands. It was to satisfy these that the company now turned its attention. The program included modernizing plants and adding manufacturing facilities to fill expanded markets for pre-war product lines. Also, it encompassed facilities to develop new processes and products which had been delayed by the war.

Another important part of the program was the expansion and improvement of research laboratories. Principal project in this field was the enlargement of the Experimental Station, on the outskirts of Wilmington (see cut on next page), at cost of some $30,000,000—Du Pont's largest single investment in research facilities.

Over-all, the program covered the most intensive period of growth in the company's history. Nine new plants, of varying sizes, were built across the

As Japan surrendered on *Missouri's* deck, Du Pont was planning new opportunities through delayed expansion.

nation. Research personnel doubled. Within five years after V-J Day, the products of the new and enlarged facilities represented 35 per cent of the company's total sales.

Man-made fibers led the way. Production of nylon increased 10-fold over 1941. Newer synthetics — "Orlon" acrylic fiber and, later, "Dacron" polyester fiber — also figured prominently in the company's advances. Neoprene synthetic rubber, plastics, agricultural chemicals, pigments, cellophane—all were produced in greater quantities than ever before.

To finance the vast program—its cost swollen greatly by advancing prices of building labor and materials—presented a problem unprecedented in the company's long history. To provide new plant and working capital (approximately 25 cents for each dollar of plant) called for large cash reserves. To help pay the bills, $100,000,000 of preferred stock was sold in 1947. Otherwise the money came from earnings retained in the business and from reserves set aside against depreciation and obsolescence.

The building was done, as it had been since 1802, under the direction of the company's own forces. The Engineering Department acted as designer and general contractor, with thousands of sub- and sub-sub-contractors participating.

The people to build and operate the plants came, literally, from the four corners of the land—key management people from older plants to accept new responsibilities; ex-farmers, bellhops, clerks, soda jerkers to man the plants and carve new careers for themselves. In the first five post-war years, the new plants created 10,000 new jobs.

BETTER TOOLS
FOR RESEARCH

DU PONT'S Experimental Station, above, is spread out on the heights above the Brandywine,* a stone's throw from the original powder mills. A $30,000,000 expansion, completed in 1951, made it one of the largest groups of research laboratories in the world.

Yet the Station accommodates less than half the company's research personnel. Altogether, there are 38 research and development laboratories spread over the na-

*On land that successively had accommodated a picnic ground, a trap-shooting club, a baseball diamond and a golf course.

NEW FIBERS include "Orlon" acrylic fiber and "Dacron" polyester fiber. Before commercial production began, $25,000,000 was risked on "Orlon." Textile industry is Du Pont's largest customer.

NEW FILMS like "Mylar" polyester film and polythene face tough competition. In wrapping material, polythene vied for customer's favor against paper, cellophane, metal foils, other plastic films.

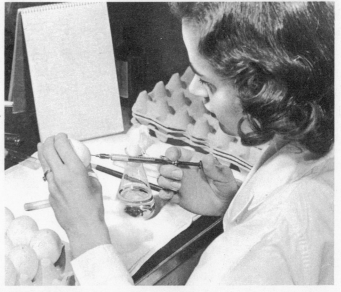

NEW FIELDS of expansion included agricultural and veterinary chemicals. Normally, 1000 research projects are under way. Odds on any one of them ringing the cash register: about 1 in 20.

tion. They are staffed by some 5000 men and women, more than 1900 of whom are technically trained; and they are financed by a research budget that now exceeds $45,000,-000 annually, about three cents of each sales dollar.

Nowadays, about half Du Pont's output represents products unknown or in their commercial infancy 20 years ago. Thus research is the company's lifeblood — the road to progress in the highly competitive chemical industry.

PRODUCTION
EXPANSIONS

NEW PLANT at Victoria, Texas, produces nylon intermediates, typifies complicated and expensive units of modern chemical industry. It is third plant built in Texas since the war.

ENLARGED PLANT at Martinsville, Va., second nylon plant, increased capacity to four times 1941 output. Seaford, Del., plant also got additions.

NEW PROCESSES were added, like the "Z" Process for making titanium pigments at the Edge Moor, Del., plant.

DU PONT TODAY

It Is a Blend Of Many Things

PEOPLE...

INDUSTRIAL production today is the effort of a team: hundreds combine skills, arts and judgments to provide a single article. The lonely Colonial craftsman's counterpart is an operator supported by a host of specialists. In Operator George Shute, front above, is focused Du Pont's entire effort—to make chemicals economically and efficiently. So complicated and involved is the process that no man could do it alone. Backing up Shute are scores* whose talents find opportunities for expression in the modern industrial pattern.

*The team: foreground, operator; left of operator, supervision; first row (left to right): carpenter, safety engineer, nurse, pipefitter, fireman; second row: control chemist, rigger, file clerk, railroad engineer, telephone operator, instrument mechanic, dye tester; third row: power engineer, stores clerk, millwright, stenographer, painter, area engineer, welder, sheet metal worker; fourth row: design engineer, electrical lineman, librarian, draftsman, blacksmith, electrician, guard. Not shown: the research teams that precede production, the sales and distribution units that bring the goods to market.

AND PROPERTIES

PLANT properties by themselves mean little; they gain significance only as monuments to man's imagination. Yet, in an industrial, technical age they are the cornucopias from which flow our material plenty.

Today, 70-odd plants and 38 laboratories operate under the Du Pont banner. Modern counterpart of the simple millstones that ground black powder are enormously complex and expensive tools like the giant chemical "spinning wheel" below, producing "Orlon" acrylic fiber at a new Camden, S. C., plant.

TECHNOLOGY

THE modern chemical industry is characterized in its physical aspects by the complexity of its tools and equipment; ratio of investment to individual employee is high. (Du Pont investment per employee: about $18,000.) Plants must be tailor-made to exacting designs, and operations require the utmost in instrumentation and control. But detractors of the modern push-button age should remember that no push-button devised the formidable apparatus above; to the last flashing light and robot recorder it is the signal creation of man.

AND TECHNIQUES

BEHIND the intricate mechanisms of the modern chemical industry is the intangible that lies only in the minds of men: the indefinable called, for want of a better name, know-how, the symbol of human resources. Accumulating over the years, know-how actually develops through endless tests and endless experimentation like that shown here: what specific combination of dyestuffs will produce, on any specific combination of textile fibers, the specific combination of color and sheen that will be precisely what the consumer wants?

VIRTUOSITY

THE vast variety of talents and skills reposing in the large modern industrial enterprise is writ in this awesome display of erudition. Placed on exhibition at the Lavoisier Library were diplomas representing 1680 degrees held by 850 technically-trained employees at a single Du Pont research location. Symbolizing the seals of 285 universities (from Harvard to Heidelberg) they covered over a hundred fields, from architecture to zoology, background for tasks ranging from creation of a gossamer fiber to the world's largest construction project.

AND VENTURE

THE model on the table here, being examined by the Executive Committee's Sub-Committee on Construction Forecasts,* is an elaborate scale representation of a chemical production unit. It cost $7000 to build. Translated into tons of brick and metal, miles of pipes and tubing it may represent an investment of upwards of $7,000,000, and yet be only a part of the plant for which it is designed. Such risks are commonplace in the chemical field; nowhere else does the meaning of nothing ventured nothing gained become quite so clear.

*Left to right: Vice-presidents Henry B. du Pont, Walter J. Beadle, Charles A. Cary.

Few companies are freer of "absentee control" than Du Pont. Board of Directors is heavily weighted with men actively engaged in management or who have retired from official posts. Monthly meeting of Board, pictured here, brings together varied talents.

JORGENSEN

MANAGEMENT

IN many aspects Du Pont management today stands in sharp contrast to its historic antecedents. The difference, however, is largely superficial; the letter, not the spirit, has changed. Today's methods reflect a conviction that a management organization is efficient only when designed specifically for its intended purpose. With this, earlier incumbents would find no quarrel.

When the company was small, personal direction was best suited to its relatively simple affairs. But to meet today's scale and complexity, the company operates on a committee principle that some students describe as radical. Power to manage the company's property and affairs lies with its Board of Directors, functioning through committees of its own membership. The principal instrument of day-to-day management is the Executive Committee, a top-level general staff which shapes broad policy. Ten manufacturing departments, aided by fourteen auxiliary, or staff, departments, carry on actual operations. The authority of Committee members is limited

Executive Committee at weekly meeting. Crawford H. Greenewalt, President, presides at far end of table. Clockwise from him are: Vice-presidents Roger Williams, Charles A. Cary, Henry B. du Pont, Walter J. Beadle, Walter Dannenbaum, William H. Ward, J. Warren Kinsman, Angus B. Echols and Committee secretary, F. G. Hess.

—decisions are reached by majority vote. The principle is that of joint or multiple judgment. The Committee is made up of men with background in various phases of the business—collectively, the synthesis represents the longest-headed and best-informed view available.

That a 9-man committee, acting on authority from a 33-man Board, can manage effectively sometimes excites wonder. To a large degree it is explained by two benchmarks of policy. First, just as the old partnership was composed of men who grew up in the mills, Du Pont's Board is made up largely of men who have spent their lives with the company. Second, most members of top management are important stockholders; owner-management is a fundamental that has survived since 1802. With enlightened self-interest so strong a factor, the company moves with rare singleness of purpose. For management conceives its first duty is to provide an environment and an incentive through which Du Pont people at all levels can find expression for their individual achievement.

Finance Committee, composed largely of elder statesmen, is responsible for all financial affairs. Left to right around table: Pierre S. du Pont (ex-Treasurer, ex-President and ex-Board Chairman), J. Bayard Eliason (ex-Treasurer), Donaldson Brown (ex-Treasurer), President Greenewalt, F. G. Hess, secretary; Chairman Echols (ex-Treasurer), Emile F. du Pont, Lammot du P. Copeland, Company Secretary; J. Thompson Brown (ex-Vice-President) and Walter S. Carpenter, Jr. (ex-Treasurer, ex-President and present Board Chairman). In rear: Treasurer T. C. Davis.

FINANCE

E. I. DU PONT DE NEMOURS & COMPANY

Average Operating Investment
1951

Cash	$ 134,886,617	9%
Marketable Securities	91,490,286	6
Accounts and Notes Receivable	118,813,053	7
Inventories	180,174,229	11
Deferred Charges	7,254,414	1
Plant and Properties	1,020,537,762	66
Average Operating Investment	$1,553,156,361	100%

Operating investment is given emphasis in reckoning performance. In calculating operating investment, Du Pont includes all working capital and plants at cost. For interesting contrasts, see page 21.

TWO basic principles govern Du Pont financial policy. First and most elementary, is to stay out of debt. This would draw a nod from E. I. du Pont, who never attained that happy state. Despite all temptations, the company has no funded indebtedness.

The second principle also derives from Brandywine days. Stated simply, it is to save part of what is earned as seed money for future development. Funds for expansion, insofar as possible, come from internal sources—reinvested earnings plus set-asides from depreciation reserves. Approximately three-fourths of the company's growth since 1802 has been financed from within; only one-fourth from new stockholder investment.

Although steeped in tradition, these policies today have little resemblance to the ultra-conservative, square-cut-spectacle financing of the Nineteenth Century. The progress of the modern chemical industry has been a financial, quite as much as a technical, achievement. The industry lives and breathes on a diet of constant change. Financially, this calls for repeated risks in behalf of new developments (see page 95) and a willingness to write off outmoded products and processes as soon as they have outlived their usefulness. It is this concept that makes the industry the dynamic force it is today.

Du Pont financial policy rests in its Finance Committee. Functionally, projects reach this group upon recommendation of the Executive Committee,* but the Finance Committee holds the strings of the purse and passes on all appropriations exceeding $300,000. It is responsible for all financial and accounting policies.

In one operating principle, Du Pont methods differ from those of many U. S. companies: it chooses to measure performance in terms of the return on investment, rather than the more familiar percentage on sales. Over a long period, this return has averaged out to just under 10 per cent. There has been many a deep valley during wars and depressions (5.6 per cent in the war year 1944, a low 2.6 per cent in the slump year 1932). This is balanced off by better records under more favorable circumstances (14.7 per cent in 1810, under E. I. du Pont; 13.3 per cent in 1950).

*Asked to describe the division of duties between these two top committees, a Du Pont official once summed it up as "we render unto Caesar those things which are Caesar's and to God those things which are God's." Which was which he declined to say.

RESEARCH

THE most important factor in Du Pont research over the past quarter-century is the broad commercial base on which it rests, with footings in a wide variety of activities. Interest in many fields greatly increases the chances of utilizing research findings. Conducting large-scale research in a single field would be like deploying a commercial fishing fleet in search of a rare aquarium specimen; the cost can be justified only when the nets can be cast far and wide. Diversity, which broadens the possibilities of a success, keeps the risks within practicable bounds.

In this way, research in lacquers and paints produced "Duco" finishes, research in rayon provided know-how that assisted in later development of nylon, nylon research begat later fibers.

Fundamental research is the keystone of Du Pont's research program (see page 99). But the majority of Du Pont effort is of necessity directed to "applied" research since industrial research must for the most part have an immediate practical goal. If it is to have meaning it must be directed ultimately toward creating something for the greater convenience, comfort or well-being of man. And this is a slow and painful process, requiring as much experience as can be brought to bear, from as many quarters as possible.

The search for new products and processes accounts for over half of Du Pont's research budget. Less spectacular is the essential, if less well recognized, development of an improved process or composition that may, in better yield or quality, shave the net cost to the consumer a cent or two a pound. Research of this kind writes few headlines and gains are noted in fractions. Yet it is the introduction of new things and new ways which has gradually pushed the American living standard upward. Only in this way can the eager U. S. consumer eat his cake and have it too.

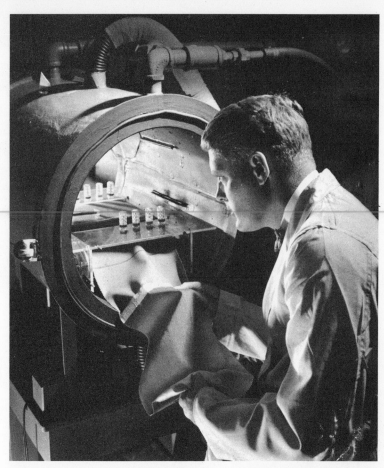

Elaborate equipment is a necessity in the modern chemical laboratory. This "iron lung" simulates effect of different weather conditions on human skin as a clue to the behavior of the fabrics now used for clothing.

Keeping up with world's scientific advances is a task in itself for modern scientists. Hundreds of technical journals are reviewed and summarized in this Du Pont research library.

Du Pont research is concerned with the problems of many different industrial fields, ranging from metallurgy to animal husbandry. Here a youthful scientist at Niagara Falls, N. Y., studies metal plating reaction.

Consumer preference registered in U. S. stores alone determines success or failure of any product, decides in long run which companies shall grow. Aim is to provide some consumer benefit far beyond its cost (dip gloves in suds instead of calling cleaner).

MARKETS

THE marketplace in which Du Pont is most at home is one calling for a key chemical material used in some universal necessity. Usually this represents a small fraction in the cost of the finished article. (The "Duco" or "Dulux" finish in the shiny surface of a car is a minor cost item; the electric refrigerator needs only 25 cents worth of "Freon" refrigerant.) How well this policy meets human needs is indicated by absorption of so many Du Pont developments into the language, habits and culture of the nation.*

This kind of market best expresses the essential relationship between business units of various sizes: a large company like Du Pont can provide economically and efficiently a product in which smaller firms can find an opportunity to create markets of their own. A nylon dress, for example, is the product of weaver, dyer, finisher, designer, cutter and retailer as much as Du Pont. (The nylon in a $49 frock costs less than $2.)

Continual opening of new markets like these, rather than exploitation of the old, is the aim. And in few is Du Pont the largest element; in many fields its competitors, though smaller

overall, lead in their particular specialties. (Union Carbide is larger in plastics, American Viscose in rayon and so on.) This is a matter of deliberate policy. To commit capital to production leadership in any one field could jeopardize development of the new products of research. Du Pont believes it can contribute most by carrying many eggs in many baskets, and adding constantly to the supply of each.

Once a new product shows signs of qualifying for a market entry, sales and merchandising forces get to work.

Sales policy is carried by 2500 salesmen with "oval" and slogan, "Better Things for Better Living — through Chemistry."

Du Pont employs some 2500 salesmen, many of them technical experts who often may be found in shirt sleeves in a customer's plant, helping to solve some difficulty. In the competitive chemical field, service is frequently a salesman's most persuasive card.

Du Pont merchandising is marshaled behind a house trade-mark or insignia which takes the form of an oval embracing the company name. It was first used in 1907 and adopted officially in 1909. It appears countless numbers of times each year on packing cases, literature and letterheads, and Du Pont salesmen are careful to have it engraved in red on their calling cards.

The slogan that frequently accompanies the oval, "Better Things for Better Living . . . through Chemistry" dates from 1935, when it appeared in a *Saturday Evening Post* advertisement and on the first program of the Du Pont radio series "Cavalcade of America," which started in October of that year. Both oval and slogan help bind Du Pont people together in a common enthusiasm; both are regarded as an assurance of a standard, and an obligation to keep the standard high.

*Foreign critics from low-living-standard countries often indict automobiles, ice-cubes, movies, cellophane wrappings and sheer hosiery as epitomizing U. S. civilization. For better or for worse, Du Pont is guilty of having had a hand in each.

COLOR

THIS remarkable Christmas morning extravaganza reveals one of modern chemistry's most cheerful achievements: the color that has penetrated the fabric of American living patterns. Consumers of a few decades ago, inured to drab and often fugitive shades for clothing, autos, home decor and knick-knacks, would have gasped at the spectacle below. Here, from a single U. S. department store (Strawbridge and Clothier, of Philadelphia) this bright rainbow of tone and tint was assembled in a random selection. And, as indicated at the right, today's parking lots are far more colorful than was Joseph's famous coat. Dyes, inks and finishes paint a pretty picture.

PHOTO BY LOEBEL

THE HUMAN EQUATION

THE corporate form of business was invented at the time of King Charles I as a means of protecting individual proprietors from pressure organizations. In modern usage, it is a charter from a state which permits a group of people to act, collectively, as an individual. Like

William E. Robinson
Is a Du Pont Employee

WILLIAM ROBINSON lives in a world completely different from the one that David Murphy knew in 1802 (see page 7), but his relationship to the Du Pont Company is still guided by the principles established 150 years ago.

Not paternalism, but individualism, was the hallmark of Du Pont's human relations in the early days on the Brandywine. Respect and concern for the individual's dignity, self-expression and opportunity were basic. Measures designed to help the individual help himself in preparing for emergencies and for the future were on an informal, person-to-person basis.

Today, because of Du Pont's size, relationships are of necessity more formal. But all spring from a fundamental conviction of mutual respect and responsibility.

Today, Du Pont employs nearly 100,000 people. The typical Du Pont employee is a substantial citizen; in his late 30's; he is married, has two children, lives below the Mason-Dixon Line. He owns his home and automobile (1947 models predominate), owns insurance policies and a savings account. Strictly in this tradition is William Robinson, an operator at the big Spruance cellophane plant near Richmond, Virginia.

Mrs. Jean Oram
Is a Du Pont Stockholder

MRS. JEAN ORAM, a widow, is one among nearly 150,000 owners of Du Pont stock, and one of more than 15,000,000 Americans whose savings have been the principal source of the dollars required to build the nation's huge industrial machine.

Some 85 per cent of Du Pont's shareholders are individuals, over half of whom, like Mrs. Oram, are women. The other 15 per cent are groups: charitable organizations, insurance and investment companies, churches, schools, estates and trusts. Through their affiliations with these groups, millions more benefit directly or indirectly from Du Pont dividends.

Widespread ownership is one of the great strengths of U. S. industry. A century ago, Karl Marx dreamed and wrote of a Utopia where the people would own the tools of production and share in their output. His dream has come true, not in the Communist state founded on the theories he propounded so ardently, but in capitalistic America.

Mrs. Oram, using her quarterly dividends* to supplement her modest income, is typical of the cross-section of Americans who own stock in U.S. corporations and share the risks and benefits of their performance.

*Du Pont has paid a dividend to its stockholders every quarter since 1903.

an individual, the corporation assumes both privileges and responsibilities: it pays its taxes, acts as a good citizen and neighbor and lives by providing useful goods.

Not the illusory and superficial index of profit, but something much more basic, measures the success of a corpora-tion. The true expression lies in human terms — how well it fulfills its obligation to employee, owner, customer and community. Management's gravest responsibility is to ad-just the rights and interests of each in adequate proportion; to keep in delicate balance the rights and interests of all.

Joseph P. Holt
Is a Du Pont Customer

JOSEPH HOLT'S firm has been a Du Pont customer for 40-odd years; just what his first purchase was he cannot recall. But today, as president of Aberfoyle Manufacturing Co., an old-line textile house, he buys large quantities of textile fibers, as well as dyes, finish-ing agents and other supplies. He spins, dyes and bleaches yarns for sale to weavers and knitters.

Thus Joseph Holt is a vital link in the business cycle which takes Du Pont materials and passes them, hand to hand, through a series of operations involving a doz-en or more firms, of all sizes, before reaching the ulti-mate consumer. The price paid for the finished article includes the value added at each successive step.

Mr. Holt is one of 75,000 Du Pont customers. Like all of them, he relies upon Du Pont service to help him with knotty technical problems. His favor is the continual preoccupation of research and production alike. For, as a customer, Joseph Holt realizes well that Du Pont research, when it produces a new development in his field, starts a chain reaction in which he is a key element. Unless he is, the chain is broken and useless; indeed, only he can determine whether or not that particular piece of research was worth doing at all.

Mayor Francis Loth
Is a Du Pont Neighbor

AS the mayor of Waynesboro, Va., Francis Loth knows first-hand the impact of a large industrial plant on a community. Since Du Pont built a $6 mil-lion acetate plant in his quiet Shenandoah Valley town in 1929, Waynesboro's population has doubled, bank deposits have risen from about $2 million to $10 million, postal receipts from $28,000 to $150,000.

The Du Pont plant has grown too: investment has increased seven-fold; production capacity is 28 times the initial unit, employment is six times greater, the annual payroll 12 times greater. (And acetate yarn that sold for $2.36 a pound in 1929 now sells, because of technological advances, for 84 cents a pound.)

Mayor Loth was a young businessman when Du Pont came to the Virginia town. He well remembers that many natives were skeptical about the new plant and the changes it inevitably would bring. But on balance, he believes, Du Pont has fulfilled the responsibilities of a good neighbor. Opportunities it has offered young people, business activity its payrolls and purchases have stimulated, taxes it has paid and its efforts to be a friendly neighbor add up, he says, to a substantial contribution to Waynesboro's welfare and progress.

THE PROBLEMS

THE problems of E. I. du Pont de Nemours and Company in 1952 were wholly unlike those which faced the company at any stage of its long history.

The problem of 1802 was largely financial, of weathering the gales that tear at any new enterprise.

The problem of 1852, when Henry du Pont had just come to the helm, was largely one of production, of effecting economies in manufacture that would permit wider distribution of his product.

The problem of 1902, when the new corporation was founded, was one of organization—of building a structure that would prepare for the modern chemical era.

Thus in each fifty-year interval there have been urgent and perplexing difficulties. They have been faced and met and eventually overcome.

These were problems, however, that could be solved by resolution, perseverance and diligence. They lay within the compass of the company's own capacities and discretion.

The problems of 1952 were not so clearly defined. For the most part these are not within Du Pont jurisdiction—they reflect the broad social and economic issues of the times.

The Problem of Bigness

There is, first of all, the problem created by changed attitudes toward bigness in business. The new sin of size figures in most indictments of U. S. industry by its detractors; their theory is that corporations reaching a certain stature should divide, like the amoeba, into segments. Otherwise, it is contended, there is no limit to the size to which large business units can grow or the "power" they can exert.

Du Pont's position is that in a competitive market size is simply a measure of usefulness; that customer preference will of itself regulate growth or shrinkage. A company will therefore attain only that size commensurate with its efficiency, and any attendant "power" will continue only so long as the company excels in service to its customers.

Du Pont defines its own function as the undertaking of those chemical assignments in which its large capital, technical and managerial resources can make a distinctive contribution. This narrows down to tackling the toughest and most complex jobs, which only a few companies have the capacity or diversity to carry through with any assurance of success. Such tasks are obviously beyond the resources of smaller firms. This is a technological fact of life which cannot be legislated out of existence.

The Problem of Anti-Trust Action

Du Pont officials have repeatedly emphasized their approval of the aims and purposes of the Sherman Anti-Trust Law and when their views have been sought have urged that it be continued intact. They have pointed out, however, that present legal interpretations of the law often have created confusion and have had the effect of overruling public interest. Weird new elements have been introduced into economics: in the post-war shortages of cellophane, a delay of nearly three years in supplying needed capacity was occasioned by a suit charging that Du Pont already had too great a share of the total U. S. output. Price reductions, which had been cheered by customers, were charged to have been harmful to the extent that they discouraged newcomers from entering the field. "It is sometimes difficult," Du Pont's president notes, "to plan the future and commit millions of dollars of stockholders' money in ventures which may, at some future date, be open to question not because they have failed but because they have succeeded."

The Problem of Markets

Du Pont products must make their way in markets which include not only other identical products but also different products performing the same functions. Some hold that competition of like versus like is the governing factor: cellophane versus cellophane, as opposed to cellophane versus paper, rubber, plastics, foil or any other material used for packaging. Du Pont experience has been that sometimes its salesmen meet stiffer competition from counterpart or alternate materials than from the direct Macy vs. Gimbel rivalry of competing firms. Thus Du Pont rayon must bid for its place both against other rayons and against cotton, wool, linen, silk or other synthetic textiles. Nylon, though until recently an exclusive and patented Du Pont product, must hold its own in a field that includes all other fibers. To contend otherwise, Du Pont feels, is to ignore the experience of the marketplace.

The Problem of Incentives

Du Pont believes that the factor of individual initiative has been the secret of American industrial progress, and is finding difficulty in maintaining it in an era of high personal income taxes. The problem is of long-range, rather than immediate concern, but the company has devoted much attention to seeking a solution.

High taxes, by narrowing the gap between income brackets, threaten to discourage the ambition to seek or accept positions of greater responsibility. As any company's most serious responsibility is to insure a succession of competent people, this creates no little anxiety.

Incentives apply as well to the investor ranks and in a degree to the company itself, particularly in periods when taxes on a basis of growth dampen enthusiasm for risky ventures into untried fields. It is felt that such measures in fact become a tax on the nation as well as the corporation by restricting, rather than expanding, its economy.

How these problems will be resolved as the company enters the sixteenth decade of its existence remains to be seen. But there is confidence in their ultimate solution. No institution can long survive unless it earns and merits the public sanction that determines success or failure. Obviously Du Pont, having endured for a century and a half, has had its measure of popular approval. Today on any issue it is content to rest its case before an American public having full understanding of the facts. Given this condition, it has no doubt or qualm about the verdict.

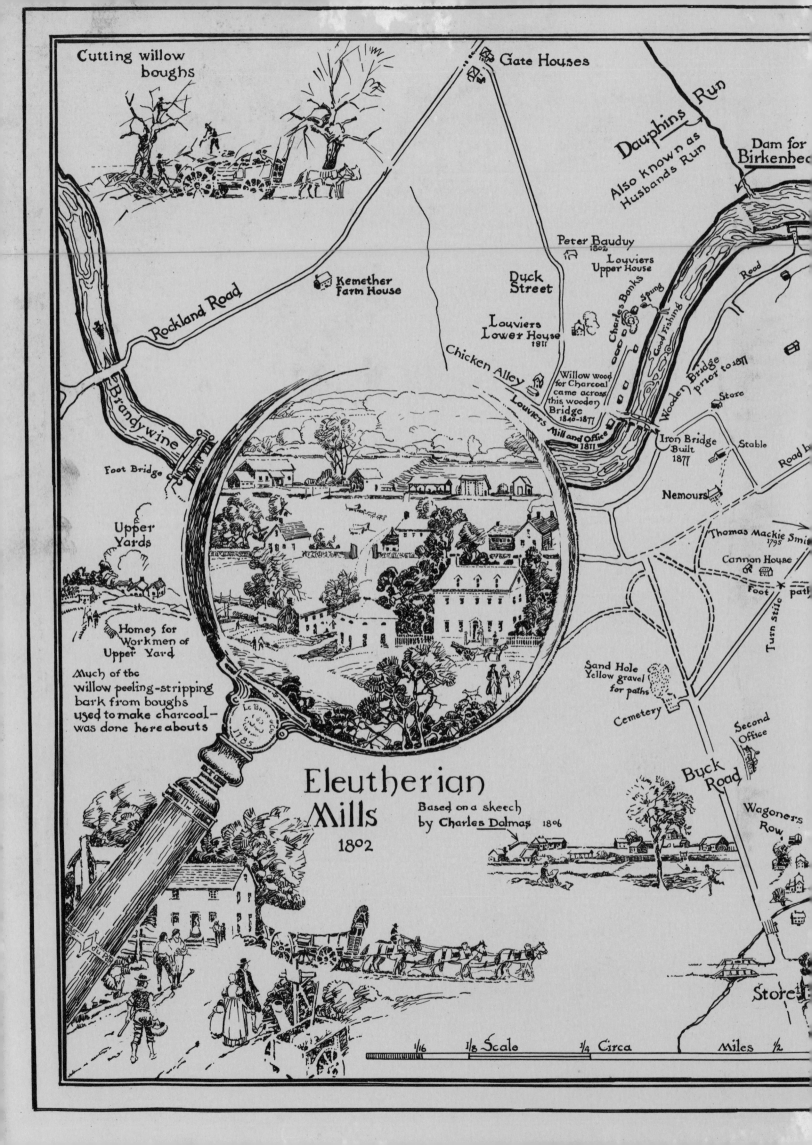

Cutting willow boughs

Gate Houses

Dauphins Run

Also known as Husbands Run

Dam for Birkenhe

Peter Bauduy 1802

Louviers Upper House

Rockland Road

Kemether Farm House

Duck Street

Charles Banks

Spring

Good Fishing

Road

Louviers Lower House 1811

Chicken Alley

Willow wood for Charcoal came across this wooden Bridge 1846-1877

Wooden Bridge prior to 1877

Store

Brandywine

Louviers Mill and Office 1811

Iron Bridge Built 1877

Stable

Road b

Foot Bridge

Nemours

Road b

Upper Yards

Thomas Mackie Smi 1795

Cannon House

Foot path

Homes for Workmen of Upper Yard

Turn stile

Much of the willow peeling-stripping bark from boughs used to make charcoal—was done here abouts

Le Barre jeune 1785

Sand Hole Yellow gravel for paths

Cemetery

Second Office

Buck Road

Eleutherian Mills

1802

Based on a sketch by Charles Dalmas 1806

Wagoners Row

Store

1/16   1/8 Scale   1/4 Circa   Miles   1/2